A Warrior's Betrayal:
The Life and Death of Green Beret Chester Garrett

By
Antonio Arias, Reynaldo Cervantes Jr., and
Eric Norway

Copyright © 2019

Angel's Trumpet Press

Antonio Arias, Reynaldo Cervantes Jr., and Eric Norway

All rights reserved. No part of this publication may be reproduced, stored in a retrieval system, or transmitted in any form or by any means, electronic, mechanical, photocopying, recording or otherwise without the prior written permission of the copyright holders, except for brief quotations used in a review.

ISBN: 9781792793578

Notice: Photographs used in this book are from the private collections of authors Reynaldo Cervantes Jr. and Antonio Arias.

Acknowledgements

The authors gratefully wish to express their thanks for help and assistance to many people. First and foremost to our supportive families, who literally make life worth living. Special thanks to Elsie, Richard, Kit and Carole for making us better writers. Our thanks to an army of law enforcement individuals from the agencies mentioned in this book and many others. Two who deserve special thanks are James Belknap for his years of leadership and wisdom, and J.W. Gee, who was haunted by this case for decades and provided incredible insight into 1970s criminal justice methodology.

Thanks to our shy Vietnamese friend who translated scores of Major Garrett's personal records and documents, and whose own story of survival during and after the Vietnam War deserves a book of its own.

Thanks to the many detectives and prosecutors we interviewed who were involved in this case for their observations and opinions.

Thanks to Major Garrett's family members for their dogged resilience; we hope this book brings some sort of closure to them. And finally, we have to say it again; the authors' grateful thanks to our families, who have supported us faithfully during our decades' long careers in law enforcement, and tolerated our countless absences from family events while "on the job."

Dedication

This book is dedicated to Major Garrett's family, whose eternal devotion and perseverance inspired investigators to bring this case to fruition, and, to the investigators whose work on this case was emblematic of the HIT Creed, "to see that justice is done, not only for the deceased, but for the surviving family as well."

A Warrior's Betrayal:
The Life and Death of Green Beret Chester Garrett

Part 1

Chapter 1

On an early Tuesday morning, January 4, 1977, John Banuelos, a nineteen year old dump truck driver for Milam Sand & Gravel in east El Paso, reported to work. It was a cold morning, mid-forties; a light but steady breeze from northwest made it feel like high thirties. El Paso has funny winters though; at four thousand feet elevation the full sun feels warm and one can usually be comfortable with just a light jacket. The dry air was crystal clear, no clouds. The far off Franklin Mountains looked closer than they actually were; a surreal effect of the rising sun in the high, dry desert.

John cranked his dump truck and let it idle a bit to warm up. Sometime after 8:00am he drove it away from Milam Sand & Gravel to get fuel down by the Rio Grande River. As he drove south on Loop 375, he saw a red Volkswagen Beetle parked in desert scrub about a hundred yards from the roadway to the west, but he didn't think much of it.

About thirty minutes later John headed back to work with full tanks and saw the Volkswagen still parked in the desert. He pulled off the road and slowly drove to the Beetle to investigate. As he climbed down from his truck, he saw a figure lying in the back seat. *Probably some drunk sleeping it off*, he thought, *too drunk to drive, pulled off the road and passed out*. John walked to the vehicle and looked in. He saw a large man crammed into the back seat of the tiny car, covered with blood. *He's dead!*

John jumped into his truck and drove as fast as he could to Milam Sand & Gravel, less than a mile away. He frantically called the El Paso County Sheriff's Department.

At about 9:20am, El Paso County Sheriff's Department (EPSD) Dispatch radioed Unit 207 to meet Banuelos at the site of a possible dead body on Loop 375 south of North Zaragoza, about three miles north of Interstate I-10. Officer L. Boyette responded and was the first law enforcement person to arrive at 9:32am. Officer Boyette confirmed the presence of a body, notified Dispatch and Captain "Mac" Stout and waited for investigators to arrive.

Sergeant Bill Rutherford showed up first. EPSD Detectives Wallace Brown and Reginald Yearwood were sent to the scene, as was ID&R (Identification and Records) Sergeant R.J. McCrea. More phone calls were made and more officers arrived. At 9:54am, Sergeant Fred Timmons and Detective John Omohundro appeared. At 10:13am, Detectives Brown and Yearwood drove up. One minute later Captain Stout, along with Detective Jesus Reyes, parked and got out.

Most of these men were from the EPSD Criminal Investigation Division's (CID) Crimes Against Persons (CAP) unit. CAP handled murders, rapes, kidnappings and other major crimes. Short-handed as always, most of the unit was present. Captain Stout was in charge of CID and answered directly to Sheriff Mike Sullivan. Sergeant Timmons ran daily operations in CAP under Captain Stout.

About this time Texas Ranger Pedro "Pete" Montemayor of the Texas Department of Public Safety (DPS) arrived.

Sergeant McCrea photographed tennis shoe prints and tire tracks as he and Sergeant Timmons worked their way to the Volkswagen. It was locked, no keys in the ignition. Sergeant Timmons was able to open the passenger's vent window and pop the door open from the inside. He retrieved a wallet lying on the floor near the gas pedal. Identification cards and photographs in the wallet matched the big man in the back seat.

"Major Chester Garrett, United States Army", Sergeant Timmons announced. The team looked at each other. *Who the hell is Major Chester Garrett?*

Chapter 2

Friday, February 9, 1968

SF CAPTAIN receives DSC

Captain Chester Garrett was presented the nation's second highest award for valor, the Distinguished Service Cross January 25 for "extraordinary heroism" while serving in Vietnam. Lieutenant General Robert York, commanding general of the post, made the presentation.

Currently commander of Company C, 5th Battalion at the U.S. Army Training Center here, Garrett served as a camp commander near Buc Dop in the 5th Special Forces Group (Airborne), Vietnam.

Garrett was cited for his actions while serving as an advisor to a Vietnamese strike force during a search and destroy mission Feb. 3, 1967. When Garrett's unit was attacked and pinned down by a North Vietnamese battalion, Garrett completely disregarded his own safety and charged an enemy position killing four soldiers who were placing heavy fire on his men.

He stood in the midst of the raging firefight and rallied his men. He then moved into the open and directed air support with a smoke grenade. Garrett led the withdrawal to a landing area and personally carried a wounded comrade more than 600 meters on his back. Again disregarding his safety, he led a carrying party back to the site and recovered the casualties before leaving the area.

Captain Garrett, 28, has been decorated 10 times for his service in Vietnam. Awarded earlier were the Silver Star, the Bronze Star, the Army Commendation Medal, the Vietnamese Honor Medal, the Purple Heart with cluster, the Air Medal, the Vietnam Campaign Medal and the Vietnam Service Medal.

Source: Veritas, February 1968

Distinguished Service Cross

On February 3, 1967, Captain (CPT) Chester Garrett led a Vietnamese Strike Force as a Special Forces Advisor. The Strike Force was on a Search and Destroy mission near the Cambodian border in Phuoc Long Province. During early morning hours, the unit was savagely attacked and pinned down by a North Vietnamese Army (NVA) battalion using machine guns, mortars and small arms.

CPT Garrett ran to the point of heaviest fighting to assess the situation and coordinate defense. He saw an enemy position manned by four hostiles and charged through a hail of bullets, killing the insurgents with rifle fire and hand grenades. CPT Garrett established a hasty perimeter and moved back to bring reinforcements forward. His South Vietnamese commanding counterpart was killed in the intense barrage and men began to falter and retreat. CPT Garrett stood amidst the raging firefight and rallied the men to fight furiously against determined North Vietnamese attackers. CPT Garrett saw two of his men against a numerically superior element, so he dashed to them and helped kill ten enemy soldiers within ten meters of their position. CPT Garrett radioed for air strikes, but pilots were unable to pinpoint the battle in the dense jungle. CPT Garrett positioned himself in the open and directed close air support with a hand held smoke grenade. Under cover of air support and artillery, he led a withdrawal to a landing zone while carrying a wounded Special Forces soldier more than 600 meters on his back. A Special Forces medic who participated in this mission recalled, "There were many wounded; it was a zoo." Again disregarding continuous heavy fire, CPT Garrett returned with a carrying party to the battle site and recovered all friendly casualties before egress.

For his actions that day, CPT Chester Garrett was awarded the Distinguished Service Cross, second highest medal after the Medal of Honor. The Distinguished Service Cross is awarded for extraordinary heroism while engaged in action against an enemy of the United States or while engaged in military operations involving conflict with an opposing foreign force.

Who the hell is Major Chester Garrett? wondered Sheriff's Department detectives on the side of the desert highway that morning in January 1977.

Major (MAJ) Chester Garrett was a highly decorated soldier

who served with distinction. In his three tours of Vietnam, MAJ Garrett was awarded the Distinguished Service Cross, Silver Star, five Bronze Stars (one with V/Device for valor), Distinguished Flying Cross, three Army Commendation Medals (two with V/Device), Soldier's Medal, three Vietnamese Gallantry Crosses with Gold, Silver and Bronze Stars, seven Air Medals and three Purple Hearts. He was posthumously awarded the Meritorious Service Medal.

However, in addition to his proclivity to earn military awards and recognition from superiors, what set MAJ Garrett apart from other soldiers was that he earned five medals for valor in a four month period. From November 1966 to February 1967, CPT Garrett earned the Bronze Star with V/Device, Army Commendation Medal with V/Device, Silver Star, Soldier's Medal and the Distinguished Service Cross respectively. What other soldiers might earn in a career, Chester Garrett did in four months.

Chapter 3

Chester Garrett was born on July 19, 1941, in Charlotte Amalie, St Thomas, Virgin Islands, to Adina Louise Francis. According to one of his sisters, Chester was a very determined and focused young man. He usually accomplished any task he set out to do. Chester constantly challenged himself physically, as was evidenced by heavy participation in team sports. He often had his sisters sit on his back while he did pushups. Chester was kind hearted and protective and seemed to have wisdom of an older soul at a very young age.

Chester's adopted father, Sidney Garrett, was in the U.S. Coast Guard. His career resulted in assignments to various U.S. Coast Guard Stations. Sidney's transfer to Puerto Rico afforded Chester an opportunity to excel in baseball. Chester was deeply passionate about the sport. Although transportation to and from baseball practice was a constant issue, Chester walked or wrangled rides from parents of fellow team members. Chester attended and graduated from Antilles High School in Roosevelt Roads, Puerto Rico in 1958. He excelled in athletics, an activity he would receive recognition for throughout his military career.

Chester was strongly recruited after high school by universities and colleges to play collegiate baseball. He declined multiple athletic scholarships and opted instead to sign a baseball contract to play professional baseball with the Chicago Cubs organization. He played a short while in the Appalachian League in 1958. Chester was a member of the 1958 Pulaski Cubs, a subsidiary of the Chicago Cubs baseball organization. His debut as a pitcher in Major League Baseball was short lived due to a sports injury. Chester subsequently focused his attention and energy to a military career. He loved his country and had a passion for being a soldier.

Chapter 4

Chester Garrett was a big man. His body was crammed into the back seat of the tiny Volkswagen with his head and torso facing forward on the floor behind the driver's seat, which was positioned fully forward. Detective Omohundro immediately realized the driver must have been a short person. The victim's legs were folded in a crouched position on the back seat on the passenger side. Chester's partially open eyes almost had a look of wonder as they stared forward at nothing.

10:14am: El Paso County Sheriff's Department Captain Mac Stout, Sergeants Fred Timmons, R. J. McCrea and Bill Rutherford, Detectives Wallace Brown, Reginald Yearwood, John Omohundro and Jesus "Chuy" Reyes were present. Texas Ranger Pedro Montemayor was there to observe and render assistance as needed.

El Paso County Sheriff's Department had an excellent CAP crew. Sergeant Timmons was a no-nonsense career man who would eventually retire as Captain. He ran CAP strictly by the book. Sergeant R. J. McCrae was a precise, detail oriented investigator who fit the role of Identification & Records Sergeant perfectly. Detective Reggie Yearwood was a former army military policeman, smart and quiet. Reggie would become the first African-American sheriff of Ector County, Texas. Detective John Omohundro was tall and slender, very intelligent, quiet and calm. Detective Jesus "Chuy" Reyes was more outgoing, social and clever. Brother of Border Patrol Chief and later U.S. Representative Silvestre Reyes, Chuy was a rising star in EPSD, becoming Chief Deputy until Sheriff Mike Davis was voted out of office. Davis' replacement brought his own managers, leaving no room for Chuy, who left EPSD and established a successful career as a private investigator.

Detective Chuy Reyes was exhausted, having been awake all night working a rape investigation. In later interviews, both Detective Reyes and Detective Omohundro described working in EPSD CAP as demanding and exhausting, but resulting in an extremely close bond between investigators. At the time, there were only five detectives in CAP who handled not only homicide, but any investigation deemed "complex", resulting in routinely working around the clock, going home just long enough to shower and change clothes. Detectives suffered from chronic fatigue and depended upon each other professionally and personally.

Captain Stout took charge and assigned Reyes, Omohundro and Yearwood to make measurements and diagram the area. Sergeant Timmons was assigned to assist Officer Reyes as Evidence Officer. Approximately 48 tennis shoe impressions were recorded, many made over the top of the Volkswagen's tire tracks. One detective observed shoe tracks that initially left the Volkswagen in a direct line to the highway but returned from an angle further south. He surmised the wearer departed southbound on the highway, probably in another vehicle, then stopped and ran back to the Volkswagen for unknown reasons.

10:45am: Detective Brown was assigned to interview John Banuelos, who explained in detail how he came to find the body.

10:58am: EPSD Dispatch confirmed the Volkswagen's license plate number and Fort Bliss sticker as registered to MAJ Chester Garrett.

11:23am: Doctor Frederick Borenstein and Medical Examiner Manuel Diaz arrived and pronounced Chester Garrett dead. A van from El Paso Mortuary showed up a short time later and transported MAJ Garrett's body to Thomason Hospital in central El Paso for autopsy. Officer Reyes continued to obtain and process evidence as other detectives completed the investigation of the crime scene.

11:50am: Detective Brown was sent to U.S. Army Criminal Investigation Division (CID) at Fort Bliss, where he met and briefed Army CID Special Agent (SA) Gary Domeny, who in turn contacted Chester Garrett's commanding officer, Lieutenant Colonel (LTC) Harrell Glenn Hall, who arrived shortly and was briefed on MAJ Garrett's death.

LTC Hall said he last saw MAJ Garrett the day before as MAJ Garrett was leaving the office where they both worked. LTC Hall advised that Chester Garrett was separated from his wife and sons; Chester lived on base in Bachelor Officers' Quarters (BOQ) building 5040, unit #19, while his family lived at 1349 Backus Street in El Paso. LTC Hall identified Garrett's wife as Lisbeth Ann Garrett and sons as Roger, age 18 and Patrick, age 12. LTC Hall also said Chester was active in sports and was an assistant coach for the Fort Bliss basketball team under head coach Lieutenant Robert Sherwin. Detective Brown asked LTC Hall to meet him at the crime scene to make a positive identification of the body. LTC Hall agreed to do so, and Detective Brown left.

12:35pm: Army CID Special Agent (SA) Jack Hall departed Fort Bliss with LTC Harrell Hall to meet Detective Brown. While en route, they were advised the body had been moved to Thomason Hospital, so SA Hall drove there instead and met Detective Brown. The investigators and LTC Hall viewed the body, which LTC Hall identified as Chester Garrett.

12:40pm: El Paso Wrecker Service towed the Volkswagen to EPSD Headquarters to be processed by ID&R. Everyone left the scene, leaving the desert to return to its quiet natural state. They all had the same question: *Who killed an army major and dumped his body in our backyard?*

2:00pm: LTC Hall and Brigade Chaplain MAJ Tom Miller went to the Garrett family house, 1349 Backus, in full dress military uniforms to break the news of Chester's death. When they arrived, oldest son Roger answered the door in a terrycloth robe. He looked at the two military officers and asked, "Oh, should I get Mom?" Ten minutes later Lisbeth came out of her bedroom wearing a matching terrycloth robe. LTC Hall told Lisbeth of Chester's death. Lisbeth asked, "Are you sure?" She asked if Chester had been found alone. LTC Hall later said Lisbeth's reaction to LTC Hall's news did not seem "genuine" and her question about whether Chester was found alone seemed odd. LTC Hall also thought it strange Lisbeth and her son would be wearing matching terrycloth robes at 2:00pm on a normal work or school day.

2:00pm: Military Police (MP) CPT Willie Lott called Army CID SA Rafael Saenz regarding a heated argument CPT Lott observed at Biggs Gymnasium on base the day before. CPT Lott was exercising at about 2:00pm when he saw MAJ Garrett enter the gym and speak to first one and then two members of the Fort Bliss basketball team. Their conversation became quite heated but not physical. The topic was unclear to CPT Lott.

2:20pm: EPSD detectives and Ranger Montemayor arrived at Thomason Hospital and examined the body. They removed clothing and processed it as evidence, noting 13 wounds, including blunt force trauma to the head and multiple stab wounds to the torso. ID&R Sergeant McCrea and Evidence Officer Manny Gurrola photographed the body, scraped under fingernails and fingerprinted the victim.

3:30pm: Lisbeth Garrett called EPSD and advised she had been visited by LTC Harrell Hall and advised of her husband's death.

3:45pm: Lieutenant Robert Sherwin called EPSD. Detective Wallace Brown told 1LT Sherwin of MAJ Garrett's death. 1LT Sherwin said he was with MAJ Garrett at about 2:30pm the day before when they had cut two basketball players, Eugene Thomas and Howard Jackson, for missing too many practices. Sherwin said, "Both men seemed disappointed in being cut from the team."

1LT Sherwin said he last saw MAJ Garrett the night before from about 6:15pm until 8:00pm when Garrett stopped by Sherwin's BOQ room to return Sherwin's car keys. They spoke about various subjects, including Garrett's upcoming transfer to Italy. Sherwin asked Garrett if he was taking his family. Garrett said he was separated from his wife and was not going to take his family with him. Sherwin also described Garrett's clothes, which were the same jogging suit, shoes and gloves he was found dead in that morning.

4:00pm: Detective Wallace Brown called Army CID SA Jack Hall and advised stab wounds were found on MAJ Garrett's body, concluding a homicide.

4:08pm: Army CID SA Samuel Altshul retrieved a key to MAJ Garrett's BOQ room at Bldg 5040 #19 and entered. He noted the lights and television were on, a half-eaten sandwich and an open can of Mountain Dew were on the table. SA Altshul called Detective Brown to report the room's condition and waited. At about 5:00pm investigators from EPSD including Captain Stout, Detective Brown, Sergeant Timmons and Sergeant McCrea, as well as Texas Ranger Montemayor and agents from the Federal Bureau of Investigation (FBI) arrived. MAJ Garrett's quarters were photographed and processed for fingerprints and evidence.

5:30pm: EPSD Detective Jesus Reyes was assigned to contact Lisbeth Garrett, inform her of the progress in the investigation, and take her to Thomason Hospital to make an identification of the body. At about 6:15pm, Detective Reyes and the Garrett family arrived. Detectives Reyes and H.Y. Gomez escorted Lisbeth to the morgue where she positively identified the body. As Detective Reyes drove the family home, he advised Lisbeth that she would have to provide a statement at some point.

6:00pm: Detective Brown interviewed MAJ Garrett's BOQ neighbors at Bldg 5040. Next door to MAJ Garrett's room was Room #20, occupied by Ethiopian Army CPT Me Gersa. The two rooms shared a kitchen. CPT Gersa said he had seen light under the door to MAJ Garrett's quarters and knew that his lights were on, but he had not seen MAJ Garrett for a few days. CPT Gersa did say MAJ Garrett had a girlfriend who once fled into CPT Gersa's room, about one month earlier, after MAJ Garrett's wife had caught the girlfriend in MAJ Garrett's BOQ room.

7:08pm: Detective Wallace Brown, Sergeant Fred Timmons and Ranger Montemayor interviewed Specialist-4 Howard Jackson, one of the fired basketball players, at the Army CID office. SP4 Jackson claimed no knowledge of MAJ Garrett's murder and gave consent for officers to search his residence at 1500 Magruder, Apt. 216, and his vehicle, a 1962 Ford Falcon located at 17001 Darrington Road in Horizon City, a suburb of El Paso. The investigators detained SP4 Jackson while they searched the apartment and vehicle, which revealed no evidence regarding murder.

11:00pm: Military Police Investigations (MPI) Section of the Fort Bliss Provost Marshal's Office called Duty CID agent SA Gary Domeny and advised of an incident from August 11, 1976, when a Private Jennifer Molina reported an incident at MAJ Garrett's BOQ room. PV2 Molina claimed she was in the room when MAJ Garrett's wife entered, assaulted PV2 Molina and threatened to kill her. SA Domeny relayed this information to EPSD.

11:40pm: Detective Brown, Sergeant Timmons and Ranger Montemayor returned to Army CID from Horizon City and continued to interview SP4 Howard Jackson. Jackson stated he had known MAJ Garrett through the basketball team since October 1976. He said he met MAJ Garrett the day before at practice when he and Eugene Thomas were cut from the team, as witnessed by 1LT Bob Sherwin. Jackson explained he went to the gym between 2:30 and

3:00pm and dressed out for basketball practice. MAJ Garrett took him aside and told him he was being cut because he wasn't taking care of team members and he wasn't coming to practice. Jackson went to the locker room, changed into his duty uniform, and returned to try to talk MAJ Garrett and 1LT Sherwin into taking him back. Another player, Eugene Thomas, was also being cut. They both tried to talk their way back onto the team, but the coaches were firm. Jackson said that "no one seemed to get upset over the matter". Jackson and Thomas stayed around for a few minutes and watched practice. Jackson asked Thomas to give him a ride home as his 1962 Ford Falcon had broken down. Thomas gave Jackson a ride home in Thomas' 1967 Fleetwood Cadillac around 4:00pm. Jackson's alibi for that evening was he stayed home, ate dinner and watched TV. He said two friends came by about 7:00pm and left about 7:45pm, after which he watched a movie until 10:00pm, when he went to sleep until 5:30am the next morning. Jackson again reported no knowledge of MAJ Garrett's murder.

Detectives had stumbled upon a dead body in the desert that morning, and at the end of the day they were able to ascertain only a few things: the victim was a high ranking army officer, married but separated, had a girlfriend who had angered his wife enough that the wife had allegedly assaulted the girlfriend, and the victim had fired two big strong basketball players just hours before his body was found. *We haven't even collected the main facts yet and we already have four suspects.*

Chapter 5

Chester Garrett enlisted in the U.S. Army as a Private (E-1) on April 15, 1960. Upon completion of basic training he attended U.S. Army Infantry Training at Fort Ord, California for qualification in his Military Occupational Skill (MOS), 11B (Infantryman). He successfully completed MOS training plus additional advanced individual infantry training through the 11th Battle Group, 3rd Training Brigade.

After infantry training, Chester was sent to Fort Campbell, Kentucky for jump school prior to reporting to his first duty assignment, also at Fort Campbell; the 2nd Airborne Battle Group, 187th Infantry, 101st Airborne Division – "The Rakkasans." Rakkasan was a term given to the 187th Infantry Regiment by the Japanese during occupation duty after WWII. Rakkasan was the closest word a Japanese translator could derive at the time to best describe airborne soldiers of the 187th Infantry Regiment. The literal meaning of Rakkasan is "falling down umbrella men."

The Commandant of USMA Preparatory School wrote a letter of recommendation for Chester's bid to enter OCS. Another army officer wrote in a similar letter of recommendation, "Every outfit Garrett is in will be the best damn outfit." Chester left a lasting impression on anyone he met or served with. He entered OCS in September 1962 and was commissioned a 2nd Lieutenant in the Infantry.

People who knew Chester have consistently said he was a person of utmost integrity. He was also full of energy, driven, straight forward, did not smoke or drink and kept himself extremely physically fit.

Upon completing OCS, Chester embarked upon the first of many military assignments and training events as an Army Officer. His experience coupled with his energetic demeanor would prepare him for multiple combat tours in Vietnam. During OCS, Chester scored high enough on the U.S. Army Aviation Aptitude Test to attend Army Aviation Flight Training.

In August 1963, he completed the U.S. Army Officer Rotary Wing Aviation Course at Fort Wolters, Texas. His aspiration to become an aviator was short-lived. During his last qualifying flight, his flight instructor failed him due to a safety violation.

In November 1963, Garrett completed the U.S. Army Jumpmaster Course. Chester's first assignment as a 2nd Lieutenant (2LT) was as a Rifle Platoon Leader with the 187th Infantry Regiment, 2nd Airborne Battle Group, 101st Airborne Division in Fort Campbell, Kentucky. 2LT Garrett had various Company Grade leadership assignments from June 1963 to November 1964, including Reconnaissance Platoon Leader, Davy Crockett ("DC", a recoilless weapon capable of firing a small tactical nuclear warhead) & Mortar Platoon Leader, Assistant S-4 (Logistics) Officer, Headquarters & Headquarters Company Executive Officer, and Battalion Adjutant and S-1 (administration and personnel) Officer. 2LT Garrett exhibited exceptional leadership. He took care of his men and accomplished tasks with energy. His Officer Efficiency Reports (OERs) reflected his physical prowess and superior oral expression.

During his assignment as a DC & Mortar Platoon leader, Garrett was given command of a weaker platoon in his company. In a short period of time, his platoon performed as well as and better than the other three platoons. Garrett accomplished this by taking personal interest in each soldier's welfare. Using his dynamic personality, he convinced soldiers in his platoon that they were better than the other soldiers in the company.

In Lieutenant Garrett's OER from autumn of 1964, his immediate supervisor noted:

> "This officer is enthusiastic, forceful and outspoken. He says what he thinks. This tendency occasionally led him into difficulty with his subordinates and superiors."

The OER endorser, the Battalion Commander, wrote:

> "Lt. Garrett is very outspoken, and initially this habit proved detrimental to his relations in the unit. I counseled this officer and noted a decided improvement.

He is intense by nature and demands the highest standards from his subordinates. He is fast developing into a truly superior officer."

While assigned to Fort Campbell, Chester met a girl named Sylvia at W.T. Grants Department Store in Nashville, Tennessee. This young lady became Chester's girlfriend, and they dated often. While they were happy, an unfortunate event occurred. Chester confessed to Sylvia that while on a temporary duty assignment at another Army post he had gone to a party and met a woman, Lisbeth. This woman was older than he and had a child. Chester told Sylvia that Lisbeth was pregnant with his child, and said Lisbeth threatened to report Chester to his commander if he did not marry her. Chester was so devastated by the news he even considered leaving the army. Chester told Sylvia he barely knew this woman and he really did not want to marry her but needed to take responsibility for his child.

Records show Chester and Lisbeth were married in September 1963, and his son Patrick Garrett was born a few months later.

In March 1965, Garrett was promoted to 1st Lieutenant. He completed the Special Forces (SF) Officer's Course in April 1965. U.S. Army Special Forces were created in 1952. SF recruits were volunteers trained to infiltrate deep into enemy territory. Paratrooper-qualified and expert in sabotage, escape and evasion, they specialized in organizing guerrilla forces to combat enemy guerrilla forces.

Chester's first overseas assignment was with the 8th Special Group Airborne, 1st Special Forces, at Fort Gulick, Panama Canal Zone, from December 1965 through June 1966. Chester served as Executive Officer of Operational Detachment A, Special Forces Airborne Company, Special Action Force, operating in Latin America. During this assignment, LT Garrett was commended for his participation in a Field Training Exercise (FTX) as commander of a detachment committed to an operational area. Chester assumed detachment command late in the planning phase as a replacement for the original Detachment Commander. His execution of various phases of the field problem was graded and compared with two other participating detachments. Garrett's composite score placed him 2nd overall.

Garrett conducted certain aspects of the operation in a "conspicuously superior manner." Noteworthy was his use of drop zone techniques and use of guerilla forces. His execution of an ambush during the FTX merited specific commendation. His first experience in Special Forces in Latin America undoubtedly enhanced his skills in conducting guerilla warfare. In June 1966, Garrett was promoted to Captain and volunteered for duty in Vietnam.

Chapter 6

EPSD Crimes Against Persons detectives in 1976. Left to right: Reggie Yearwood, Wally Brown, John Omohundro, Chic Gomez and Jesus Reyes

Early next morning, January 5, 1977, the detectives were back at it again. A known constant in homicide investigation is when a body turns up no one gets much sleep for a few days.

6:30am: ID&R Sergeant R. J. McCrae photographed the Volkswagen and processed it for latent fingerprints.

8:10am: Detective Wallace Brown, Army CID Special Agent Jack Hall and CPT Steven Orrison (appointed as Summary Court Officer) met at Army CID to coordinate recovery of MAJ Garrett's personal property at his BOQ, office, and gymnasium lockers.

8:30am: Dr. Frederick Borenstein performed the autopsy at Thomason Hospital. Detective Wallace Brown was detailed to observe. Dr. Borenstein concluded his autopsy report as follows:

ANATOMICAL DIAGNOSIS:

1. Blunt injury fracture of skull with

severe contusion of brain

2. Numerous stab wounds with hemothorax on left side and small wounds in the diaphragm and left kidney.

OPINION:

It is the opinion of this examiner that this man died of the injuries received, specifically the injury to the head. This injury is compatible with some survival, perhaps even several hours. The stab wounds are probably inflicted post mortem, mainly because I have seen no evidence of aspiration of blood. Admittedly, the amount of blood is rather large for post mortem bleeding, and perhaps this stabbing took place in the terminal phase.

8:30am: EPSD Captain Mac Stout received a call from Army CID Special Agent Anthony Lirette, who said that Defense Investigation Service (DIS) SA Claudia had some information on Chester and Lisbeth's marital problems, discovered when DIS conducted a background check for Garrett's Top Secret clearance renewal.

9:00am: Sergeant Timmons, Detective Omohundro and Ranger Pete Montemayor met with Army CID Special Agent Lirette and DIS Special Agent Claudia at Fort Bliss. SA Claudia said he learned from LTC Harrell Hall that Chester and Lisbeth Garrett separated before September 25, 1975 and Chester moved into BOQ. Chester had told LTC Hall that Lisbeth accused him of infidelity and publicly embarrassed him numerous times. Lisbeth had complained to LTC Hall that after an unnamed officer and colleague of Chester's died, Chester was using the dead officer's car and sleeping with his wife. Chester had likewise complained to LTC Hall that Lisbeth had sent one of his sons to spy on him on post.

SA Claudia further related that during MAJ Garrett's background investigation, he interviewed First Sergeant Joe Hawkins, who told SA Claudia about an issue MAJ Garrett had with Sergeant First Class George Martin, a mess sergeant in the dining facility MAJ Garrett commanded. SFC Martin told 1st SGT Hawkins that MAJ Garrett interfered with SFC Martin's handling of a problem with an unnamed female cook under SFC Martin's command, and MAJ Garrett was having an affair with that female cook.

9:20am: Private First Class Eugene Thomas, the other basketball player fired by MAJ Garrett, arrived at Army CID after being directed there by his chain of command. PFC Thomas seemed shocked upon learning of MAJ Garrett's death. He agreed to return for an interview at 11:00am, and when he did he was asked to return at 12:30pm as investigators were busy processing Chester Garrett's personal items.

Sergeant Timmons, Detective Omohundro and Ranger Pete Montemayor located MAJ Garrett's lockers at Bundy Gymnasium and Center Gymnasium, cut off locks and took custody of their contents. They went to MAJ Garrett's office and met LTC Harrell Hall. LTC Hall advised them that while MAJ Garrett was a staff officer at ADA School Battalion, he was also in charge of a dining hall at Fort Bliss. LTC Hall said a few days before his death, MAJ Garrett had "severely chewed out" a cook in that dining hall, Private Roosevelt Hill. LTC Hall said PV1 Hill was a problem soldier who had multiple arrests by El Paso Police Department (EPPD) for illegal possession of weapons, had recently been court martialed and was pending a Bad Conduct Discharge.

While Detective Brown searched MAJ Garrett's desk contents, LTC Hall engaged office clerk Specialist-5 Joseph Hammond in conversation. SP5 Hammond had worked with MAJ Garrett for at least two years and knew him well. SP5 Hammond advised that MAJ Garrett was romantically involved with soldier Jennifer Molina and Molina frequently called looking for MAJ Garrett, sometimes using phony names or attempts to disguise her voice. SP5 Hammond said her last call was a few days before Christmas 1976. When SP5 Hammond told her MAJ Garrett was not in, she said, "I'll kill the son of a bitch!"

10:11am: Sergeant Timmons, Detective Omohundro and Ranger Montemayor met 1st SGT Hawkins at the School Battalion. 1st SGT Hawkins said when SFC Martin came by his office one day, Hawkins asked him how he and MAJ Garrett were getting along. SFC Martin said MAJ Garrett interfered with his management of a female cook, and SFC Martin suspected she and Garrett were having an affair.

10:25am: CPT Resen of Fort Bliss Staff Judge Advocate called EPSD Detective Reginald Yearwood and said he had a young lady in his office with information about MAJ Garrett's murder. A few minutes later, Detectives Yearwood and Reyes met with CPT Resen and Private First Class Jennifer Molina, who said she was "going with" MAJ Garrett. Detective Yearwood requested to transport PFC Molina to EPSD for an interview. CPT Resen agreed and sent 1LT Elaine Anderson along to escort PFC Molina.

11:10am: EPSD detectives interviewed PFC Jennifer Molina. Molina said she had arrived at Fort Bliss in October 1975 after basic training for Advanced Individual Training (AIT) as a Nike Missile Mechanic, and was "seen together quite often" with MAJ Garrett from October 1975 until February 1976, although "at this time we were no more than friends." Molina was unsatisfied with her training course and in January 1976 complained to MAJ Garrett, who arranged to remove Molina from Student Battalion and reassign her to A Battery, HQS Command. Molina noted, "It was automatically assumed MAJ Garrett and I were more than friends."

Molina said that on February 6, 1976, she heard a rumor about her implied relationship with Garrett, became angry and went to see Garrett at his office at Battalion HQS, Bldg 1020, at about 5:00pm. In her words, "We talked and laughed about this statement, it began to get dark, one thing led to another and a relationship started." They traded telephone numbers and later met for the first time in his BOQ room. From that point on they had a steady relationship.

Molina said she stayed in Garrett's BOQ room over Easter 1976, and "Mrs. Garrett" starting calling the room every five minutes beginning at midnight until Garrett finally disconnected the phone. By then Molina knew Garrett was married but in the process of getting a divorce. Molina said that about a week later Garrett discovered his "assets were frozen and what wasn't frozen was gone", including some $16,000 in a credit union account closed by Lisbeth.

Molina said that in June 1976, she took a trip home to California to see her father and sister. Molina had left some valuables, including checks, in Garrett's BOQ, along with some clothes. Apparently, these items were discovered by Lisbeth, because Molina said Mrs. Garrett confronted her at her workplace, accompanied by her younger son Patrick. Molina denied having a relationship with MAJ Garrett, and Lisbeth told her, "Get your Goddamn boots on; you're going to get wet." Lisbeth told Molina to get her stuff out of MAJ Garrett's BOQ by 4:00pm or they would be gone. Lisbeth also told Molina she better never catch Molina there again or Molina was "good as dead". When Molina met with Garrett that night, "anything of value was gone". Garrett told Molina that Lisbeth had taken all of his plaques, achievement awards and trophies from his BOQ. Molina noted that Garrett had a bump on his head and welts on his back. Garrett told Molina that Lisbeth had hit him on his head with a board or a baseball bat.

Molina said after that incident she and Garrett cooled off their relationship and didn't see each other for a few weeks until mid-July 1976 when Molina moved back into Garrett's BOQ. On August 10th Molina had CQ Duty, requiring her to stay awake all night. Next morning she went to Chester's BOQ room and slept. About 2:00pm, oldest son Roger broke into the room, followed by Lisbeth and Patrick. Molina said they threatened her and beat her with a belt and a clothes iron until she passed out. When she woke she called Garrett, who came over and discovered they had taken his wedding ring, OCS ring, a scout knife and all of his personal checks. Molina went on sick call, called the MPs and filed assault charges against Lisbeth.

Molina said the next incident occurred on August 29, 1976. Garrett left her alone in his BOQ to play baseball in Ysleta, a neighboring town. Thirty minutes after he left, Mrs. Garrett and her two sons broke in again. Lisbeth told her to start talking and added that she was "a crack shot". Molina, fearful of another beating, chose to cooperate with Lisbeth, who told Molina she wasn't the first girl Chester had gone out with, and Chester was just using her. Lisbeth told Molina she had a good mind to kill her and let "Chet" find her in his room dead. Lisbeth said she wouldn't hang for it; he would. She ordered Molina to put on her shoes and told her they were going to take Molina to the ballgame where Chester was playing.

When they arrived, they walked towards Chester, and Lisbeth put her arm around Molina and said, "Isn't this cozy, his wife, his mistress and his children all to watch him play baseball." Chester saw them approaching and Lisbeth said, "If he dies of heart failure,

I'll buy you a steak dinner." Lisbeth told Molina to stay away from Chester, because something bad was going to happen to him, and she told her to not quote Lisbeth because as far as Lisbeth was concerned it was never said.

After the game, Chester met them in the stands. Lisbeth asked Chester, "Are you going to marry this young lady, because if you are, I want to be there tomorrow when you stand there in front of General Lunn, or are you going to come home with me and the kids and we will go to Italy in April?" Chester told Lisbeth he would go home with them and asked her not to make a scene. Lisbeth drove Molina to the BOQ where her car was parked and told her if Molina wanted Chester, it was fine with Lisbeth if Molina wanted a corpse for a husband, because that's what he would be when she was done with him. Chester Garrett moved into the house with his family but told Jennifer Molina to move into his BOQ room until he returned. After a few days Chester and Lisbeth again went their separate ways, and he and Jennifer lived together again in BOQ.

Molina said the last time she saw MAJ Garrett was on December 15, 1976. Around 10:45pm that night Molina was alone in his BOQ. Lisbeth came to the door and rang the doorbell. Molina heard Lisbeth fumbling with a key in the locked door. Molina grabbed her purse and went into the kitchen. MAJ Garrett's neighbor, the Ethiopian officer in Room 20, let Molina into his room from the kitchen. While CPT Me Gersa watched from his window he described to Molina that it was a pretty lady with a pistol in her hand. Lisbeth entered Garrett's room and left after a few moments. Molina stayed at CPT Gersa's BOQ until Garrett arrived. Garrett sent Molina to her enlisted quarters and said he would call her, which he did not do.

Molina said Mrs. Garrett called her at work again, threatening to take Molina to court and get her thrown out of the army. Mrs. Garrett demanded a sworn affidavit from Molina, and told her again to stay away from the BOQ. Molina said the conversation upset her so much she took her key to MAJ Garrett's BOQ and gave it to her company commander, CPT Joseph Rozman.

Molina said she flew home to California on annual leave for Christmas and New Year's and returned on January 3, 1977, about midnight. She went to Fort Bliss without her luggage and stopped by the BOQ. Garrett's room lights were on, but he wasn't home. She got a ride from a co-worker, Charles Hicks, and returned to the airport to retrieve her luggage. They stopped for a drink at the Knight's Club. She returned to her quarters about 2:00am and went to work the next day as usual. Molina learned of Garrett's death from Hicks about 6:00pm that night, January 4, and watched it on the news at 10:00pm. Molina's interview concluded, and she and 1LT Anderson returned to Fort Bliss about 5:30pm.

10:45am: Detective Jesus Reyes gathered, processed and submitted a list of evidence taken from the Volkswagen into the case file.

11:00am: Detective Wallace Brown met CPT Steven Orrison at Army CID to collect MAJ Garrett's personal effects, including several papers from Garrett's desk at Bldg 1020. While property was being inventoried, CPT Orrison told Detective Brown that MAJ Garrett was close to a "Mrs. Juarez", a civilian worker at the dining hall MAJ Garrett commanded.

12:00pm: Detective Brown interviewed CPT Isaac Diggs about Private Roosevelt Hill. CPT Diggs said he learned from one of his cooks, SGT James Martin, that on January 3, MAJ Garrett "verbally corrected" PVT Hill for being out of uniform. SGT Martin told CPT Diggs that PVT Hill became visibly upset but controlled himself. CPT Diggs said he spoke to PVT Hill later that evening about his encounter with MAJ Garrett, and PVT Hill responded that he would "seriously hurt someone" if given the opportunity.

1:55pm: Detectives Wallace Brown and John Omohundro finally interviewed Private First Class Eugene Thomas about being kicked off the basketball team. PFC Thomas gave consent to allow them to search his barracks room and vehicle, a 1967 Cadillac Fleetwood. Thomas denied anything to do with MAJ Garrett's death. Thomas stated he met MAJ Garrett in September 1976 when he tried out for basketball and confirmed that 1LT Bob Sherwin was primary coach and MAJ Garrett was assistant coach. On December 22, 1976, the team played a game at Eastwood High School and MAJ Garrett benched Thomas for the entire game because Thomas had missed several practice sessions. Thomas said he quit the team that night until January 3, 1977. On that day he called MAJ Garrett at his office and asked if he could come to practice. Garrett initially told him no, but then said if Coach Sherwin said Thomas could rejoin, he would accept Sherwin's decision. PFC

Thomas went to the gym at 2:00pm and dressed out for practice. Thomas said MAJ Garrett and Coach Sherwin arrived between 2:30pm and 3:00pm, so Thomas went to talk to them. Coach Sherwin did not take Thomas back because MAJ Garrett had already decided to cut him. Thomas believed 1LT Sherwin did not want to go over the head of a Major. Thomas changed into his military uniform and watched the practice with another player, "a guy named Jackson", who had also been cut. They watched for a few minutes and left. Jackson didn't have a car so Thomas drove him to his house and went to his barracks. At 6:00pm he reported for extra duty (punishment for being AWOL on December 28, 1976) and was released at 7:15pm. He located his friend David Smith; they went to Jon's Club on North Loop Road and met a couple of girls they knew. They all returned to the barracks so Thomas and Smith could change into better clothes and went to a Howard Johnson hotel for the night.

2:45pm: LTC Harrell Hall called Army CID SA Samuel Altshul and said PV1 Roosevelt Hill was currently at the dining facility, Bldg 1006, with a bandage over one eye, threatening people and acting hostile. LTC Hill advised he was sending Hill's commanding officer, CPT Isaac Diggs, to Army CID to speak with SA Altshul. CPT Diggs arrived a few minutes later and repeated what LTC Hill had told them about the encounter between MAJ Garrett and PV1 Hill, and added it occurred the morning of January 3. SA Altshul contacted EPSD Detective Brown, who requested that Army CID detain PV1 Hill so Detective Brown could interview him.

3:10pm: Army CID Special Agents Altshul, Hall, and Dehart went to the dining facility, apprehended Private Hill, transported him to CID and turned him over to Detective Brown for questioning.

Detective Brown briefed the agents of the autopsy results: MAJ Garrett was probably killed by a blow to the back of his head that fractured his skull in three places; he was also stabbed numerous times in his torso while unconscious or dead from the head trauma. Detective Brown also said SP4 Jackson and PFC Thomas were still regarded as suspects, although their alibis had thus far checked out to be true, and they were cooperating. Detective Brown attempted to interview Private Roosevelt Hill, but Hill refused to cooperate or give consent to have his home or vehicle searched.

At the close of the second day of investigation into MAJ

Chester Garrett's murder, detectives had discovered besides his wife Lisbeth being angry with him, apparently both she and Chester's girlfriend Jennifer Molina might be capable of violence against him, Chester likely had another girlfriend named "Mrs. Juarez", and a disgruntled army cook was now a suspect along with two basketball players.

The final official event on January 5, 1977, was probably a letter the commanding officer of Fort Bliss Air Defense Academy, Colonel Russell McGraw, sent to "Mrs. Chester Garrett", 1349 Backus, El Paso, Texas 79925. The letter reads:

> Dear Mrs. Garrett,
>
> It is with great sadness that I learned of the recent loss of your husband. I realize that words cannot express one's true feeling at such a time. However, let me offer my deepest sympathy on behalf of all of us in The School Brigade in your moment of bereavement.
> Sincerely,
> RUSSELL M. MC GRAW
> Colonel, ADA
> Commanding

Chapter 7

General Westmoreland, LT. Hau, CPT Garrett, March 1967

Chester Garrett began his first combat tour to Vietnam as an advisor in Regional Forces/Popular Forces (RF/PF) Operations Detachment B-34 in Phuoc Long Province.

While in Vietnam, SF Colonel Francis J. Kelly developed a strategy known as Mobile Guerrilla Force, in which bands of some 200 men -- a team of two officers and nine enlisted Green Beret soldiers and South Vietnamese soldiers and civilian irregulars -- set out on long-range patrols. They were expected to remain in the field for several weeks to gather intelligence and spring ambushes, but often had to be withdrawn prematurely because of supply problems.

American Advisors were assigned to RF/PF detachments to train Vietnamese forces for combat. The RF was local militia units organized within each district in South Vietnam to engage in offensive operations against local Viet Cong (VC) forces. RF units were better paid and equipped than PF units and could be assigned duties anywhere within the home district. Popular Forces on the other hand, were South Vietnamese National Guard-type local military units. American military forces referred to RF/PF as "Ruff-Puffs."

Garrett was responsible for advising the Province Chief on the deployment of more than 2,000 RF/PF troops. Garrett had to prepare and train RF/PF troops for combat. He improved administrative support for his soldiers, resulting in the first time RF/PF soldiers were paid regularly and on time. They were also issued authorized clothing that had been hoarded on the shelves of sector warehouses. Garrett greatly increased morale by increasing construction of RF/PF dependent housing and initiating a RF/PF food supplement program in the Province.

Garrett worked closely with his Vietnamese counterparts to establish a scheduled training program for soldiers on defense against organized VC and NVA forces. Garrett planned numerous combat operations with his Vietnamese counterparts against known enemy troop concentrations. Local RF/PF units conducted small scale operations which met with immediate success.

Garrett's initial OER in Vietnam noted, "CPT Garrett participated in many combat operations with his RF/PF units and has been recommended for the Vietnamese Cross of Gallantry. CPT Garrett has done an outstanding job during the short span of this report to improve the overall effectiveness of the RF/PF Program within the Phuoc Long Province", and "He exhibited a brand of leadership and example that spurred his counterpart - the (Vietnamese) Sector Commander - to accomplishments rarely achieved."

Garrett participated in several combat patrols with the B-34 Reconnaissance Platoon. This platoon was known as the "Apaches" and Garrett was designated "Chief" by his fellow SF soldiers. The Apaches' mission was to confirm intelligence reports on Viet Cong activities and to set up ambushes of opportunity. Civilian Irregular Defense Group (CIDG) forces participated in operations with Detachment B-34. CIDG forces received six weeks of advance training before becoming platoon members.

SP4 John Roberts, a former platoon advisor, said, "Night missions can be a problem because we have to increase our security and even a cough can carry a long way, and heaven forbid a lighted cigarette. If we run into an ambush, there's only one thing to do: Return fire and try to break through the ambush."

In order to successfully spring ambushes against Viet Cong, Apaches used the element of surprise, heavy firepower and claymore mines to "reduce the number of enemy combatants."

The mission of a CIDG camp was to train strike forces and

village defenders, bring local populace under South Vietnamese governmental influence, utilize paramilitary forces in combat operations to reinforce organized hamlets, carry out interdiction activities, and conduct joint operations with Vietnamese Army units when such operations furthered CIDG efforts. Members of CIDG also conducted psychological operations to develop popular support for the government. They established an area intelligence system including reconnaissance patrols, observance posts, and agent informant networks and established border screens along the Cambodian and Laotian borders.

In one early Detachment B-34 operation, Garrett was able to convince the Dong Xoai Subsector Commander to allow his RF company to participate in a four day combat operation, resulting in five VC killed. Garrett's ability to advise Vietnamese in an effective manner and his demonstrated leadership prompted his selection to command SF Camp A-341

In November 1966, CPT Garrett transitioned to Detachment Commander of SF Camp A-341, Bu Dop, Phuoc Long Province, Republic of Vietnam. SF Camp A-341 was the northernmost Camp in Phouc Long Province located approximately four kilometers from the Cambodian border and approximately 90 kilometers north of Saigon. SF Camp A-341 was in a remote and isolated location in relation to other friendly forces.

Garrett's CIDG force consisted of three American officers and 11 enlisted men, all Special Forces, while his CIDG was comprised of approximately 500 Stieng Montagnards. He employed CIDG forces to aggressively patrol his assigned tactical area of operations. Garrett was tasked with conducting surveillance of 50 kilometers of common international boundary between Cambodia and South Vietnam with a mission of preventing enemy infiltration.

When Garrett assumed command of SF Camp A-341, it was considered to be a mediocre unit. It took Garrett just five months to mold A-341 into one of the best "A" camps in Vietnam. Garrett instilled an aggressive approach into his Lac Luong Dac Biet (LLDB – Vietnamese Special Forces) counterparts and their CIDGs to interdict VC and NVA infiltration routes into their area from Cambodia. Garrett's initial approach to prepare the CIDG units for combat was infantry and patrol tactics training. He advised the

District Chief in civil affairs, psychological and military operations. The District had a population of 5,000 people. Garrett also advised in training and tactical deployment of RF/PF troops. Garrett revamped local district intelligence nets. He supervised training of new intelligence agents and organized new nets that soon collected timely and accurate information.

Garrett patterned his operations to quickly react to this intelligence by organizing quick reacting reconnaissance platoons to locate enemy forces. He followed through with well-planned larger operations to pursue enemy forces until contact was made. Enemy forces encountered were destroyed with available artillery and air power. His methods gained quick results, and in a five month period Garrett's CIDG forces made contact with estimated enemy forces of company, battalion and even regimental size a total of nine times. In one of these engagements, they captured numerous enemy documents, described by intelligence specialists as one of the biggest of the war. Garrett's local district intelligence nets were a major factor in inflicting massive casualties against enemy forces.

SF Camp A-341's area of operations was the site of frequent significant enemy contact. According to Chester's commander, frequent enemy contact was due to Garrett's exceptional tactical ability and his aggressive search for enemy components. Garrett repeatedly achieved outstanding tactical results while sustaining a minimum number of friendly casualties.

In late 1966, intelligence indicated North Vietnamese units had established a north-south infiltration route ten miles east of SF Camp A-341. This route was heavily used from October through December 1966 by the newly formed 9th NVA Division. In early 1967, Garrett's forces made several significant contacts against that division, which resulted in over 400 enemy casualties. Garrett's commanders noted Garrett employed his forces with great tactical effectiveness and demonstrated a high degree of professional competence. He was particularly adept in the use of tactical air support, as engagements usually took place well outside of range of any friendly ground support artillery. These engagements resulted in capture of enemy documents which provided information of significant value, including confirmation of infiltration of the 9th NVA Division.

Garrett was so successful that his command post at SF Camp

A-341 was visited by a number of very senior officers, including General William Westmoreland, commander of all American forces in Vietnam. Garrett personally briefed General Westmoreland on results of his engagements in March 1967. General Westmoreland was very complimentary of Garrett's tactical successes. Garrett remained at SF Camp-341 until May 1967, where his command was among the most active and most effective of 70 SF Camps.

It was during his command of SF Camp A-341 during November 1966 to February 1967, where Garrett accomplished what can best be described as his five moments of valor, earning the Bronze Star w/V Device, Army Commendation Medal w/Valor Device, Silver Star, Soldier's Medal and the Distinguished Service Cross respectively.

Without access to veterans who had served with Chester Garrett in war time, a good indication of his state of mind was through his OERs obtained at that time. The most detailed OER CPT Garrett received during his first tour of duty in Vietnam reflected the time period between November 1966 through April 1967, while Garrett was Commanding Officer of Detachment A-341, in which his commanding officer wrote:

> "Captain Garrett has performed as commander of a Special Forces 'A' Detachment in a combat zone in a truly outstanding manner. With an extraordinary display of fortitude and the application of sound leadership practices, he has taken what was a mediocre command and molded it in five months into what is now considered the best all around "A" camps in Vietnam. This officer has developed a new approach to find and fix the enemy. He instilled in his LLDB counterparts and their CIDGs an aggressive approach to the stated mission of interdicting the VC and NVA infiltration routes into the province from Cambodia. He first revamped the local district intelligence nets and supervised the training of new agents. He organized new nets that soon began to collect timely and accurate information. He patterned his operations to quickly react to this intelligence by organizing quick reacting reconnaissance platoons to locate the enemy and then

followed through with well-planned larger operations to pursue the enemy until contact was made and finally destroying him with all available artillery and air power. His methods gained almost immediate results and in the past five months his CIDG forces have been in contact with estimated enemy forces of company, battalion and even regimental size a total of nine times. In one of these contacts the unit captured enemy documentation which was termed by several intelligence specialists as one of the biggest find(s) of the war. Captain Garrett has taught by example as well with several extraordinary displays of heroism in the face of the enemy for which he has already been awarded the Silver Star with other decorations pending, both American and Vietnamese. His tremendous physical strength and indomitable courage has saved the lives of three whom he carried on his back under direct enemy fire to an area where they could be evacuated by helicopter. Since he took command of this detachment he has been responsible for the complete renovation of the camp defenses. He has planned and initiated the construction of a new refugee hamlet that had been pending for months prior to his arrival. He has improved the living standards of the CIDG soldiers and their dependents which has resulted in a high camp morale. One of his most noteworthy achievements has been the excellent rapport he has established and maintained throughout with his sub-sector counterpart, the district chief. Through his close association with this important official in the Vietnamese political chain-of-command, he has been able to initiate several projects directed at benefiting the people and the Revolutionary Development program for the district. The district chief has readily accepted Captain Garrett's advice in matters affecting the employment of subsector military and paramilitary forces in securing the district against and destroying local VC infrastructures. This sometimes brash young officer will leave behind him in this command a string of success that will be difficult to beat. With the benefit of additional formal education, Captain Garrett will without a doubt continue this outstanding performance in positions of greater responsibility and requiring higher rank. This officer should attend his career course as soon as possible."

Army OERs are filed annually on army officers or whenever an officer has accomplished a feat of brilliance warranting a special OER. Garrett's war time OERs are so superlative it is obvious his commanders were in awe of the man. There is no doubt Chester Garrett's very identity was as a warrior and no doubt combat was this man's purpose for living.

Chapter 8

On January 6, 1977, at 8:47am, EPSD Detective Reginald Yearwood interviewed CPT Edward Zazenski, PFC Jennifer Molina's new commanding officer. CPT Zazenski said the key to MAJ Garrett's BOQ that Molina gave to former commanding officer CPT Joseph Rozman in December was returned to MAJ Garrett on Monday, January 3, by CPT Rozman.

At 9:25am, PFC Jennifer Molina returned to El Paso County Sheriff's Department headquarters to continue her interview with her female escort, SSG Rene Rivera. She was interviewed by Sergeant Fred Timmons and Detectives Jesus Reyes and Gayle Garress. After consenting to having her quarters and vehicle searched, Detectives John Omohundro and Yearwood transported Molina to Fort Bliss and searched her vehicle as witnessed by Army CID Special Agent Jack Hall, PFC Molina and 1LT Elaine Anderson. They then returned to the sheriff's office for her interview. PFC Molina opened by stating this was her second statement and she wished to add several things.

Jennifer Molina said that in June 1976 she had a friend, Specialist-5 Magruder, who worked in the same office as MAJ Garrett, and he had witnessed incidents between Mr. and Mrs. Garrett. SP5 Magruder advised Molina to break off her relationship with Garrett because "somebody was going to be snuffed", and went on to say Mrs. Garrett was out of her mind.

Molina referenced her assault by Lisbeth Garrett on August 11, 1976, and said she was assaulted with a clothes iron and a belt. She watched Roger and Patrick rummage through MAJ Garrett's desk drawers and saw Patrick take a knife from its sheath and a class ring with a blue stone while Roger took MAJ Garrett's checkbook. Lisbeth took MAJ Garrett's wedding band from the same desk, looked at Molina and said, "I hope you don't mind if I take this; he won't need it." Roger added, "He better not come around the house, or I'll shoot his ass off."

Molina said she was asleep when they entered and woke as they were going through MAJ Garrett's desk. She said Mrs. Garrett took a clothes iron from the closet and a belt from the dresser drawer and said, "I'm going to leave some battle scars on you; what you need is a good beating." Lisbeth beat Molina with both items as the boys watched from the bedroom door. Patrick offered his mother the knife he had taken and said, "Here, Mom, use this." Lisbeth ignored Patrick and continued to beat Molina until she passed out.

Molina said when she awoke the iron and belt were on the floor. She called Garrett, who came to the BOQ. Chester told her Roger was at his office waiting to talk to LTC Hall. He loaded her car with her belongings and sent her to her enlisted barracks. Garrett called her that night and said, "Ann and the boys are seeing a psychiatrist; they're crazy." Molina said around this time frame Garrett told her that one time the wife of a First Sergeant "Krebbs" or "Krepps" went to MAJ Garrett for assistance. Lisbeth saw them together and rammed her car into the woman's left rear fender on purpose. At that point Molina's second interview was concluded.

At about 3:00pm, Specialist-4 Charles Hicks agreed to go to EPSD to be interviewed by Detective John Omohundro.

SP4 Hicks said he met Jennifer Molina in October 1976, and they went out a couple of times but "just didn't hit it off". Molina told him about being threatened by Mrs. Garrett and how her tires and vinyl car top were slashed once. Molina immediately suspected Mrs. Garrett or her sons. Hicks knew Molina had a relationship with MAJ Garrett and had a key to his BOQ, but he also knew she had turned the key in to her commanding officer in December. She was angry with MAJ Garrett at times and complained to Hicks that he never intended to leave his wife. About two months earlier, Hicks said, Molina was with him in a parking lot and they saw MAJ Garrett looking at them. Molina put her arms around Hicks and kissed him to make MAJ Garrett jealous. Hicks said, "That's when I noticed how big he was." Hicks verified Molina's alibi for the night of January 3, that he picked her and her luggage up at the airport when she returned from annual leave.

At 6:30pm, while EPSD detectives canvassed the Backus Street neighborhood, Sergeant Timmons spoke to Mr. and Mrs. John Wentzel, who said they had had repeated problems with the Garrett boys. Mr. Wentzel said while Mr. Garrett was polite, concerned and attempted to correct the boys, Mrs. Garrett overruled him each time in front of the Wentzels.

Chapter 9

On January 7, 1977, EPSD Sergeant Fred Timmons contacted Orba Malone, Lisbeth's attorney, requesting Lisbeth and her sons give statements and consent to search their residence and vehicles. Mr. Malone advised he had conferred with Lisbeth, who did not wish to give a statement nor cooperate with investigators at that time.

El Paso FBI Assistant Special Agent in Charge (ASAC) Thomas Westfall received an anonymous telephone call from someone he suspected was a white male around fifty years old. The caller stated he wanted to provide information on Chester Garrett's murder. He stated MAJ Chester Garrett was a supplier of narcotics to a group of military "pushers" at Fort Bliss. The caller said cross-border drug trafficking had become more difficult, and Garrett attempted to "jack up the prices to the pushers, and this led to the pushers snuffing him", after which the pushers stole Garrett's stash of drugs. The caller stated his source told him Garrett was involved in a large narcotics transaction in Big Bend National Park when a "Customs Patrol" informant was killed in a shooting. The caller abruptly hung up.

EPSD Detective Jesus Reyes was called by El Paso Police Department (EPPD) Detective Joe Rios, who advised he was called by a Mrs. Johnson who claimed to have information of Chester Garrett's murder and asked that officers meet her at her home in El Paso at 9:00am the following morning.

Sergeant Fred Timmons obtained Grand Jury Subpoenas to collect medical and psychological records pertaining to Lisbeth, Roger and Patrick from William Beaumont Army Hospital and telephone records for 1349 Backus from Mountain Bell Telephone. He gave the subpoenas to Detective Wallace Brown to serve.

MAJ Chester Garrett's funeral took place at Fort Bliss National Cemetery at 1:45pm. Lieutenant Colonel Harrell Hall gave the eulogy and later remarked it was one of the hardest things he'd ever had to do in life. LTC Hall orated:

"We are gathered here in memory and in honor of Major Chester Garrett. Chet Garrett was born on July 19th, 1941, in Saint Thomas, The Virgin Islands, and died January 4th, 1977, at El Paso, Texas. He is survived by his wife, Lisbeth Ann, two sons, Roger and Patrick, his mother and father, two brothers and three sisters. Chet began his military career in 1960 when he enlisted for three years in the Regular Army. He immediately established the pattern he was to follow throughout his career by seeking out the most dangerous and challenging duty available. His first assignment was to the 2d Airborne Battle Group, 187th Infantry, 101st Airborne Division, at Fort Campbell, Kentucky. The quality of Chet's service as a young Airborne soldier is reflected in his nomination to attend the United States Military Academy Preparatory School at Fort Belvoir. Chet excelled at the Preparatory School but was unable to obtain an appointment to the Military Academy. He persevered in his ambition to be a commissioned officer, however, and in 1963 was admitted to the Infantry Officer Candidate School at Fort Benning. After graduation from OCS and commissioning as a second lieutenant, he returned to Fort Campbell as a rifle platoon leader.

"In 1965, as the conflict in Southeast Asia intensified, Chet volunteered for duty with the Special Forces, and shortly thereafter received orders for Vietnam. During the period from 1965 to 1973, Chet served three tours in Vietnam and another with the Joint Casualty Resolution Center in Thailand. His service in Vietnam included duty as Special Forces Advisor, 'A' Detachment Commander, Infantry Company Commander, Battalion S-3, Battalion Executive Officer, and 'C' Detachment Executive Officer. It was in Vietnam that Chet Garrett earned his reputation as one of the fiercest and most courageous fighters in the entire United States Army. He was totally dedicated to winning the war, and he was brave to the point of recklessness. He routinely drove himself to the limits of physical endurance and regularly risked his life in a maximum effort to find and destroy the enemy. Chet's courage, leadership and immense strength were reflected in the nickname his admiring contemporaries affectionately bestowed upon him--the Chief. Ground support fighter pilots are said to have stayed on station or returned for additional strikes in response to a call that 'the Chief's in trouble' or 'the Chief needs help'. For his service in Vietnam, Major Garrett received the Distinguished Service Cross, the Silver Star, the Distinguished Flying Cross, the Soldier's Medal, five Bronze Stars for Valor, eight Air Medals, the Joint Service Commendation Medal, three Army Commendation Medals, three Purple Hearts, two Vietnam Crosses for Gallantry with Palm, and numerous American and Vietnamese service medals and unit citations.

"After returning from Southeast Asia in 1973, Chet was assigned to the Department of Tactics, United States Army Air Defense School, and from October 1974 until his death, he served as Executive Officer, Student Battalion, The School Brigade. In this final assignment, Chet was known best for his high standards of performance and his overriding concern for the welfare of the individual soldier. He derived his greatest satisfaction from helping a young soldier to overcome a personal or career problem, and he devoted countless hours of his off-duty time in doing so.

"Chet Garret was a completely uncommon and extraordinary man. No one who came into contact with him could fail to be affected by his great strength of character, his contagious self-confidence, and his unswerving faith in his nation and in the United States Army. He was known and admired throughout the Army by general officers and privates alike. He was a hero of the first magnitude, a soldier's soldier, a warm compassionate man, and a loyal friend. This officer recently commented, 'When the shooting starts, I want

Chet Garrett on my right flank.' There is no higher tribute that any soldier could receive.

"The loss of Chet Garrett will be keenly felt, not only by his family, his hundreds of friends, and his unit, but by the entire United States Army. All who came in contact with him are better for having known him. Those of us who knew him well may consider ourselves especially fortunate. We are not likely to meet his equal."

Chester's sister Cheryl remembered the song "Hail to the Chief" being played in his honor, due to Chester's military nickname being "Chief".

Investigative efforts continued while Chester's funeral was underway. EPSD Sergeant Timmons gathered three EPPD reports regarding the Garrett family. One report was filed by neighbor John Wentzel complaining about vandalism to his house suspected to be committed by Roger and Patrick. Another was called in by Chester when two bicycles were stolen from their garage.

A third report was filed by Lisbeth against Chester on July 14, 1976. Details of the complaint stated that Lisbeth claimed that Roger had just finished playing in a baseball game when Chester punched him in the face. Responding police officers noted a "small red mark" on the right side of Roger's jaw.

Also on January 7, Detective Wallace Brown interviewed CPT Joseph Rozman, PFC Jennifer Molina's former commanding officer. CPT Rozman said that in September 1976 he became aware PFC Molina and "a Major Garrett" were having an affair. CPT Rozman was concerned because Molina was his responsibility, so he spoke to her several times about any problems she might be having. Molina finally told CPT Rozman of her affair with MAJ Garrett. Molina also told CPT Rozman of her assault by either MAJ Garrett's wife or son. CPT Rozman conferred with Molina's supervisor, CPT Gooch, and pieced together that she had been assaulted with a clothes iron. CPT Rozman said he believed the affair had already ended based on conversations with PFC Molina in September 1976.

On the same day, Detective Wallace Brown interviewed Erlinda Juarez, a civilian worker in the dining hall. Ms. Juarez said she first met MAJ Garrett in October 1974. In 1975, Ms. Juarez' son, also a soldier, was charged with AWOL. MAJ Garrett interjected himself into the process and greatly assisted her son. Shortly after, Erlinda Juarez and Chester Garrett became romantically involved. She was divorced and knew Chester was divorcing his wife. She heard a rumor in the dining hall that MAJ Garrett was dating a female soldier named Molina, but it didn't bother her. Ms. Juarez said she never asked MAJ Garrett about his personal affairs, and he never asked of hers. She last saw him privately on Christmas Eve 1976 when she visited him at his BOQ. She last saw him publicly the morning of January 3, 1977 in the dining hall; they spoke about Chester helping her get post vehicle stickers for her car. She learned he was killed the next day. She ended her statement: "I have no idea who would want to harm Major Garrett; he is always trying to help people and goes out of his way to help a person in need."

Chapter 10

Bronze Star V/Device

CPT Garrett's first award for valor was the Bronze Star w/V Device. He earned this award on November 28, 1966, while serving as a Special Forces Advisor to a platoon size Vietnamese unit on a search and destroy mission near Thuan Kiem. It was early morning and thick haze was cast over the terrain. When Garrett and his men prepared to cross a rubber plantation, intense machine gun fire erupted from approximately 50 meters away on their left flank and pinned down the lead group. Garrett, who was advising the rear element, deployed his men forward to establish a base of fire in support of the pinned lead men. He disregarded steadily increasing Viet Cong fire and ran from one position to another urging his men to advance and to maintain continuous fire into enemy emplacements. On the strength of his group's suppressive fire, the lead element attacked the Viet Cong and Garrett added his men to the assault. Garrett and his men attacked the enemy from right, left and center. Garrett led the charge at center. Garrett and his men maneuvered into the enemy's rear area and completely overwhelmed the Viet Cong.

The Bronze Star Medal is awarded to any person who, while serving in any capacity in or with the military of the United States after 6 December 1941, distinguished himself or herself by heroic or meritorious achievement or service while engaged in an action against an enemy of the United States or while engaged in military operations involving conflict with an opposing foreign force. Awards may be made for acts of heroism which are of lesser degree than required for the award of the Silver Star.

Chapter 11

On January 8, EPSD Detective Jesus Reyes called Mary Johnson to follow the lead provided the day before by EPPD Detective Joe Rios. Mrs. Johnson told Detective Reyes she knew a girl, Barbara McCoy, who worked at Sunland Park Racetrack, who knew a girl who was dating MAJ Chester Garrett. Mrs. Johnson didn't want Barbara McCoy to know she was talking to police, but she knew that Barbara McCoy knew this other girl very well. Mrs. Johnson also said she knew MAJ Garrett had been at a Christmas party on December 14, 1976, with this other unknown woman.

Coincidentally, EPSD Detective Wallace Brown researched names in MAJ Garrett's office phone directory and found two to be significant, "Jerrie Pletcher" and "S. Turner". He determined "S. Turner" was Sharon Turner of Sunland Park, New Mexico.

Detective Brown contacted Sharon Turner and interviewed her at her home. Sharon said she was introduced to "Chet" Garrett on September 17, 1976, through her friend Jerrie Pletcher. She and Jerrie went to the Rodeway Inn on Interstate I-10 in El Paso and coincidentally met Garrett there. Sharon Turner was going through a divorce and had recently returned to the El Paso area, living with her parents in Sunland Park. Chet called her the following day and they started dating. Garrett would take her to dinner or visit her at her parents' home. To Sharon, Chet Garrett seemed to be a good Christian man. They often talked about God together. She never suspected he was married nor had a family. Once or twice while out to dinner they ran into Chet's sister Cheryl. They did not attend any functions at Fort Bliss; they usually went to dinner and returned to her parents' home to visit. Sharon denied ever having sexual relations with Chet, because of her religious convictions, although he wanted to. She wanted their relationship to be based on Christianity instead of sex. Chet and Sharon spoke of marriage; her divorce would be final in January 1977, he was transferring to Italy, so they planned to marry and she and her children would go with him.

The last time Sharon saw Chester Garrett was on Sunday,

January 2. He told her he had been receiving crank phone calls that day. Chet picked her up, and they drove around El Paso and Las Cruces, New Mexico, looking at houses. Chet told her he wanted to buy a house to rent out before they left for Italy so they would have a place to live when they returned from overseas.

Sharon spoke to Chet the last time by telephone the next day, Monday, January 3 at about 8:30pm. They usually spoke twice a day, and earlier, but Chet called later this day because after basketball practice he realized he still had Lieutenant Sherwin's keys. Chet took them back to the Lieutenant, and they chatted for about ten minutes. Chet told her he was going to bathe and go to bed. He said he would visit her the next day, and they hung up.

Detective Brown asked her about a red Volkswagen music box. She said it was a Christmas present from Chet to her son Cory. She concluded the interview by saying, "Chet did not have anyone that would want to hurt him that I knew of."

While Detective Brown was interviewing Sharon Turner, EPSD Detective H.Y. Gomez was interviewing Mrs. Jerrie Pletcher. She and her husband J.J. had lived in El Paso for about six years. She met and befriended Sharon Turner, who had two children, Connie, 14 and Cory, 4. Sharon was going through a divorce from Benny Turner.

Jerrie Pletcher said she and Sharon met MAJ Chet Garrett on September 17, 1976, at the Knights Club at the Rodeway Inn of El Paso. Sharon and Chet danced and became acquainted and started dating after that night. They visited Jerrie's house several times. Chet impressed Jerrie as being well-educated and polite. Jerrie said neither she nor Sharon knew Chet was married with children until after his death. Jerrie said the last time she saw Chet Garrett was when he and Sharon attended a Christmas party with the Pletchers at Sunland Park Racetrack around December 15.

Detectives Jesus Reyes, H.Y. Gomez and Wallace Brown arrived at 1349 Backus for a scheduled interview with Lisbeth Garrett. Her brother, Roger Gilman, a soldier stationed in Germany, showed the detectives in and said Lisbeth would be out in a few minutes. Twenty-eight minutes later, Roger Gilman told the officers Lisbeth did not feel well enough to talk with them at this point.

On January 10, 1977, El Paso FBI ASAC Thomas Westfall received a second anonymous telephone call from the same man who had called on January 7 about Chester Garrett's death. The caller again said Garrett "was snuffed because he tried to jack up the price of drugs" that were getting harder to smuggle into the United States because of increased border inspection. The caller claimed "contacts" provided information to him about people furnishing "uppers and downers" to kids' softball teams. The caller hung up. ASAC Westfall took notes and provided them to the investigators:

> "Joseph Nelson is military, living at Fort Bliss. His wife Liz worked at Taylor Publishing Company of Dyer Street in El Paso. Another girl named Carol or Caroline who worked at Taylor Publishing was married to a military guy. They belonged to a swinger's club and swapped husbands and wives. They divorced and she started dating a black MP; she is white. The people, including Carol, in the swinger's club are involved in narcotics. E-6 Edward Courtois and his wife Kathleen are in the club and sell drugs. Courtois was a life guard at 13th Ordinance Company at Fort Bliss. They move him around because he steals army supplies. On April 1, 1975, he stored stolen goods at a house that consisted of three cots, an adding machine, a typewriter, 15-20 black note books, 15-20 white note books, two electric drills, and a tent. His wife Kathleen admitted this. Two MPs help Courtois move the supplies on and off post. There is also a minister named Wally Chapman and his wife that are involved in the sex deals. He has a church on Alabama Street. The stolen property is sold to support their drug habits."

That afternoon, Detective Sergeant Fred Timmons received a telephone call from Doctor Frederick Borenstein, who estimated Chester Garrett's time of death as the evening of January 3 before midnight, and the cause of death being the blow to the back of the head. A two inch by two inch piece of skull was broken away, conducive to the weapon being a baseball bat or similar.

On January 12, 1977, Army CID SA Hall interviewed MP Heide and MP Leniger, who were conducting security duty at the Fort Bliss Robert E. Lee Gate from 6 pm until midnight on January 3. Neither remembered MAJ Garrett or his red Volkswagen Beetle, but Heide remembered a conversation with a woman, possibly Lisbeth, in a white Continental in late December.

Also on January 12, Detective Wallace Brown interviewed Sharon Turner about her and Chester Garrett's activities on New Year's Eve day and New Year's Day. Sharon said Chet came to her home on New Year's Eve between 7:00pm and 7:15pm and they visited with her parents until about 9:00pm, when she, her daughter Connie, and Chet went in Chet's Volkswagen to St. Clements Church in El Paso. They participated in a church New Year celebration until about 2:00am when Chet took them home. Sharon said the next day, New Year's Day, at about 5:00pm, Chet called Sharon to say he was coming over later. He arrived at her and her parents' home about 6:30pm, had dinner and stayed until about 1:00am.

Chapter 12

Silver Star

On December 9, 1966, Captain Chester led a 25 man Vietnamese reconnaissance platoon on a mission from Special Forces Camp A-341 to the Cambodian border along the Dok Hoyt River. Garrett and his men were trying to locate a crossing site for future operations and to verify presence of a large North Vietnamese Army (NVA) unit in the area. Garrett and Specialist-4 Marion Cartlidge, the only two Americans on this mission, were with the main body of troops when the point man abruptly walked into an NVA bivouac area. Garrett knew friendly forces held the advantage over the surprised enemy and led a charge into the camp. The NVA force responded with heavy automatic weapons and mortar fire. Garrett continued forward and engaged seven or eight NVA soldiers armed with AK-50 and Chinese carbines. Specialist Cartlidge saw him kill two NVA soldiers with his rifle in a point blank exchange of fire. His aggressiveness inspired the platoon, and together they assaulted and overran the nearest entrenched enemy, causing the rest to retreat.

The disorganized enemy fled east from the bivouac area, dragging wounded with them, but left six dead behind. Garrett withdrew the platoon into a defensive perimeter. He suspected a strong counterattack and organized an airstrike on the enemy position via radio, but the aircraft were several minutes away. Although the friendly force was just a 25 man platoon facing a superior numerical force, CPT Garrett remained in place to direct and assess the air strike, which he did while under fire. After the airstrike, Garrett and his men moved back in, still under sporadic enemy fire, to collect documents and destroy whatever food and munitions they could not carry out. In all, Garrett and his men killed six enemy soldiers and wounded seven while an estimated 15 additional enemy were killed by the airstrike. Intelligence derived from captured documents yielded that he had attacked elements of the 308th Battalion, part of the 52nd NVA Regiment. CPT Garrett's immediate action and competence under fire were direct factors that led to success of the reconnaissance patrol with no injuries.

The Silver Star is awarded for gallantry in action while engaged in action against an enemy of the United States or while engaged in military operations involving conflict with an opposing foreign force. Actions that merit the Silver Star must be of such a high degree that they are above those required for all other U.S. combat decorations but do not merit award of the Medal of Honor or Distinguished Service Cross.

Chapter 13

Thursday, January 13, was a big day for the detectives and the District Attorney's Office. After avoiding cooperation with law enforcement since Chester's body was found on the January 4, Lisbeth Garrett and Roger Garrett were forced by court order to appear before the Grand Jury of El Paso County about their knowledge of the matter. In attendance were Jim Butts and John Cowan of the District Attorney's Office and Sergeant Fred Timmons of the El Paso County Sheriff's Department.

Lisbeth was first to testify. John Cowan advised her of her Miranda rights, and questioned her about her and Chester's marital issues. Lisbeth stated that while she had filed for divorce a year earlier, nothing had been done legally as they attempted reconciliation. She painted a picture of Chester being affected by his wartime experiences as the reason for their relationship problems. "Since the first time he went to Vietnam probably", she said, "Chester had a problem adjusting back to family life. You have to realize that he was a highly trained military man. Extensively so. He was an intensive man and it was difficult to turn this off and come back to family life at times, and this is what we had worked with for several years. Well, when he came back…when the peace treaty was signed he went to Thailand and when he came back he just…well, he was just very keyed up, you know."

Lisbeth stated Chester had two residences; his family home and the BOQ, and he split his time between them "50-50". She was vague and seemed uncertain about when she saw and spoke with Chester on January 3, but said his visit and calls were in reference to an upcoming visit by Colonel and Mrs. Comee, family friends from Fort Bragg. She testified when Chester arrived at their home, son Roger moved Chester's Volkswagen from the driveway into the garage so he could "shoot some baskets."

At one point Assistant District Attorney Cowan asked, "Mrs. Garrett, would it not be fair to say that you and your husband were still having a lot of marital problems and were not getting along as late as January 3, 1977?"

Lisbeth responded, "No. I think it would be fair to say that we had gotten, had reached the point where he had decided that we would have our life together in Italy and it had, it had smoothed out quite a bit."

Lisbeth became testy and evasive during the following exchange:

> Q-"To your knowledge he (Chester) did have a girlfriend who was a WAC at Fort Bliss?"
> A-"Well, my husband told me she was the girlfriend of his...not roommate, but there's an apartment type thing with a kitchen in the middle and this is what he told me."
> Q-"All right. Let me ask you this. Were you aware of the fact that your husband had told another woman that he was going to take her to Italy with him?"
> A-"I am certainly not aware of that, no."
> Q-"I would like to direct your attention back to on or about the twenty-third day of June last year. I realize that it is difficult to look back and think about dates when they are that far back, but if you will try your best we will certainly appreciate it."
> A-"Yes."
> Q-"Do you recall going to the BOQ with Roger, your son Roger, and threatening this lady, Molina?"
> A-"No."
> Q-"Beating her with a belt and a clothing iron?"
> A-"No."
> Q-"You don't recall any of that?"
> A-"No, that didn't happen."
> Q-"All right. So you are denying that in June you did go into your husband's BOQ and beat this woman, Molina?"
> A-"Yes, I certainly am."
> Q-"Okay. Now, referring to somewhere around the last part of August, you do recall going

into the BOQ and finding Ms. Molina there, do you not?"

A-"Yes."

Q-"And do you recall telling her that you were going to take her to the ball game where your husband was playing baseball in Ysleta?"

A-"No. I was told that she was the roommate's girlfriend. All right. The clothes were there and she was there and I simply asked her if she would like to go to the ball game with us and she said yes, she would enjoy it very much. So she did."

Q-"Okay. So you did take this lady, Molina, to Ysleta with you, is that correct?"

A-"Yes."

Q-"When you got to Ysleta your husband was playing baseball?"

A-"Yes."

Q-"And did you ask your husband in the presence of other people whether or not he was going to marry Ms. Molina?"

A-"No one knew who she was. I suppose…she just came and I just came down in the bleachers and let them talk. I wouldn't say that in front of anyone."

Q-"I take it that you also did not tell Ms. Molina that you had a good mind to kill her and let your husband, Chester, find her dead in his BOQ so they would blame it on him?"

A-"No, of course not."

Q-"Did you tell Ms. Molina at that time if she knew what was good for her she would stay away, that she had better stay away from your husband?"

A-"No, I did not."

Q-"Did you go to your husband's BOQ as late as December 15 of last year?"

A-"I could have. I have a key to his BOQ."

Q- "Okay."

A-"Which he gave me."
Q-"Did you know that Ms. Molina was there when you went into the BOQ?"
A-"When is this?"
Q-"On the...last month on December 15, 1976."
A-"No."
Q-"Did you have a pistol? Did you ever have a pistol out at the BOQ?"
A-"No."
Q-"Do you own a pistol, ma'am?"
A-"No, my husband does."
Q-"Do you have one at home?"
A-"My husband has his military pistol."
Q-"Do you know what caliber it is?"
A-"Yes, I do. It's a P-38."
Q-"And you never have gone to Fort Bliss with that pistol?"
A-"No, of course not."
Q-"Or any other pistol?"
A-"No, of course I have not. He keeps the pistol in with his things. He also has several rifles and other things."
Q-"Did your husband ever give you that P-38 and tell you that he wanted you to keep it?"
A-"No."
Q-"So it is your testimony that if this lady, Molina, accuses you of having assaulted her at the BOQ last year that she would be either mistaken or lying? Is that correct?"
A-"Yes, she is. She is very much so."
Q-"Okay. Mrs. Garrett, will you give the Sheriff's Department the consent to search your home, your garage and your automobiles?"
A-"Yes."
Q-"Will you give them a full, written statement?"
A-"Yes, I have no objection to that."

ADA Cowan moved into Lisbeth's activities the night Chester was killed. Lisbeth testified Chester arrived at the Backus house about 7:45pm, and only she and Roger were home after taking Patrick and a friend to the movies. She said she and Chester discussed the upcoming visit of family friends from Fort Campbell, Kentucky while Roger played basketball in the driveway. ADA Cowan confirmed with Lisbeth that Roger drove Chester's Volkswagen into the garage to make room for him to "shoot baskets" in the driveway. Lisbeth was unable to specifically answer ADA Cowan's questions about Chester's contact with Roger during that visit, inside the house, garage or on the driveway, but she did say she and Roger saw Chester off from the driveway as Chester drove away in his Volkswagen around 8:15pm or 8:20pm.

Lisbeth was excused and Roger Garrett took the stand. John Cowan advised Roger of his Miranda Rights and began questioning him.

Roger testified he was in the dining room playing with an electric racing car set he had received for Christmas when his father came to the door on January 3. Roger let Chester in through the front door. After looking at Roger's car set and making small talk, Chester went through the living room into the kitchen with Lisbeth, and they moved into the family room to talk. Roger said he went outside, moved his dad's Volkswagen into the garage and shot fifty to seventy-five basketball free throws. When he finished he went inside, heard his parents talking about family friends coming to visit, and got himself a snack. His parents came out of the family room and all three exited to the driveway through the garage. Roger said his father adjusted the driver's seat back to how he liked it, got in his car and left.

John Cowan changed the subject to Jennifer Molina.

> Q- "Okay. All right. Now, Roger, your mother told us about an incident that occurred out at the BOQ where she found this lady by the name of Jennifer Molina in your father's BOQ, and she said that you were with her. Is that correct?"
> A- "Yes, sir."
> Q- "And she also said that Pat was with her; is that correct?"
> A- "Yeah."
> Q- "And do you recall when that happened?"

A- "Well, it was some time ago. I know that it was during baseball season."

Q- "It was sometime in August. Would it have been sometime in August?"

A- "Yes, sir, summer, when we were playing summer ball."

Q- "Okay. Do you recall seeing this lady's clothes there in the BOQ?"

A- "Yes, sir, I have seen them in the closet."

Q- "And do you recall you and your mother taking some of your father's personal items from the BOQ at that time?"

A- "Well, just his knit socks, his pull ups, you know, because he forgot them."

Q- "Okay. Have you ever seen a knife that your mother talked about that has the engraving that says Chester Garrett III?"

A- "Well, I don't remember the engraving, but he had knives and daggers from ranger schools and awards and achievements on plaques and stuff and, you know, around the house. It's just stuff he brought home."

Q- "Okay. Didn't you all take some of those plaques that date?"

A- "I don't think so. I am not sure. I can't be sure. I really don't know."

Q- "What did your mother tell this lady when she found her there?"

A- "She just asked her if she would like to go to baseball game."

Q- "Okay. Was that all she asked her?"

A- "She asked her what she was doing there, but I guess that was fairly obvious."

Q- "It wasn't any secret to your mother or you what she was doing there, was it?"

A- "No, sir."

Q- "In other words, your mother knew that your father had been going out with this girl, is that right?"

A- "Yes, sir."
Q- "And that she was living there?"
A- "Yes, sir."
Q- "And it would be fair to say that your mother was pretty upset about it like she told us?"
A- "Yeah, it upset her, but I think it is something she accepted because, you know...I don't know."
Q- "Now Roger, I realize this isn't easy for you and it wasn't easy for your mother, but your mother and your dad just flat weren't getting along, were they?"
A- "That's not correct. Okay. There were periods a year ago when the divorce proceedings started where...well, Mom told me the reason the divorce was in process was, you know, she had to do something to get Dad to come around. And I know as a fact since this summer that things have been running smooth at the house. It was my first year of baseball and Dad coached me and we worked maybe eight hours a day together on just talking baseball and, you know, the mental preparation and then on the field, you know. We talked, you know, baseball all day and practiced three, four, five hours a day. We got kind of close this summer. It was kind of funny. He's a former professional player and he coached me and I won individual honors and stuff. Patrick is an all-star. Everyone in the family was, you know, geared into baseball and we all got closer because of it and Dad was coming over a lot more and we were getting along and we all wanted to go to Italy and stuff like that. It was running real good."
Q- "Do you...what exactly did you see your mother do to the lady when she caught her there at the BOQ?"
A- "She just talked to her."
Q- "All right. Now, Roger, you understand it's important for you to shoot straight with us?"
A- "Yes, sir."
Q- "And that you have got to tell all the truth?"
A- "Yes, sir."

Q- "All right. I am referring to the time that she caught her at the BOQ and there was quite an incident that occurred there that your mother has told us about."

A- "I didn't really know that there was any real big incident. Not, you know...they may have talked but I didn't see anything big go on."

Q- "You didn't see your mother assault this lady?"

A- "No, sir."

Q- "Did it seem strange for her to say 'Let's go to the baseball game together' to you?

A- "Well, what she wanted to do was...my father was at a baseball game. He had a game that day in his league. And the purpose was to deliver, give my father a choice, you know. Does he want to live...what kind of lifestyle does he want? Does he want his family or does he want to go on the way he has been? And that was the option left open. And that was the last time I heard anything of Ms. Molina."

Q- "Right. In other words, your mother wanted to try to give him an ultimatum, 'Either you take her or you take me.' Wasn't it something like that?"

A- "Of sorts, yes, sir."

ADA Cowan clarified a couple of small technical points and dismissed Roger.

The use of a Grand Jury to elicit a confession is risky. The Grand Jury process itself is controversial. It is used solely to benefit the prosecution, be it a District Attorney's Office or a federal United States Attorney's Office. A Grand Jury is comprised of a large group of jurors, sometimes as many as fifty. The same Grand Jury meets weekly or monthly to hear any cases brought before it by the District Attorney's office or U.S. Attorney's Office for several months at a time. Proceedings are managed by one of the prosecutors, who presents witnesses to explain facts of the case. The Grand Jury considers evidence presented by witnesses and issues a "True Bill" if they believe a crime has been committed, or a "No Bill" if they believe evidence presented is flawed or insufficient.

Defense attorneys despise the Grand Jury system because they are not allowed to participate. Defense is generally not allowed to even attend Grand Jury proceedings, nor allowed to have an opportunity to contest the evidence nor cross examine the witnesses. In fact, Grand Jury proceedings are often sealed and defense counsel has no access to testimony or evidence presented unless the case goes to trial. To defense attorneys, the Grand Jury system is so one-sided in favor of the prosecution that a running joke is "you can indict a ham sandwich" before a Grand Jury.

Normally, the Grand Jury is a vehicle used to secure indictments and generate arrest warrants against specific defendants. It tends to be a "rubber stamp" operation; a detective or police officer testifies to a quick litany of facts, a juror might ask a question or two to clarify a particular point, the witness is dismissed and a True Bill is issued. The pace is quick as the Grand Jury may have to hear scores of cases each session. A vote of "No Bill" is extremely rare.

To present a witness other than law enforcement is unusual, and that witness is usually either an informant testifying against a defendant, or a subject matter expert used to explain a complex issue. To present a defendant like Lisbeth or Roger to a Grand Jury, apparently in an attempt to secure a confession, is a risky move by prosecutors. If the Assistant District Attorney (ADA) succeeds in securing a confession while the defendant is on the stand, the case is essentially over; prosecutors win. If the defendant obviously lies before the Grand Jury, jurors will usually issue a True Bill and indict. Perhaps the District Attorney's Office felt odds were in their favor to gain a confession from one or both of them, since Lisbeth and Roger were not polished career criminals and appeared generally unsophisticated. The danger in this tactic is upon failure to secure a True Bill, the case is dead in the water unless new evidence is discovered that can be presented to a later Grand Jury. In retrospect, presenting Lisbeth and Roger to Grand Jury proceedings only nine days after the violent murder of their husband and father was not a good idea. The jurors were still under the influence of the initial shock of the crime and were possibly more sympathetic to family members. No incriminating physical evidence was presented. This Grand Jury issued a No Bill in the case of Chester Garrett's murder.

However, as Lisbeth promised during her Grand Jury appearance, that afternoon EPSD detectives obtained a statement from her and Roger as well as consent to search her home and vehicle, in the presence of her attorney Mike Cohen.

Chapter 14

Soldier's Medal

On January 2, 1967, Captain Garrett was serving as Special Forces Advisor to a Vietnamese unit during a combat mission at the Song Be River near the Cambodian border. As the men crossed the river, one soldier slipped and was rapidly swept downstream by the strong current. In spite of his heavy gear and clothing, CPT Garrett jumped in and swam to the drowning man, reaching him about 100 yards downstream. Although the struggling soldier dragged him under twice, CPT Garrett was able to secure the soldier's rifle and gear and swam him back to shore. CPT Garrett was awarded the Soldier's Medal for saving the young man's life.

Constant rain in Vietnam caused rivers and streams in SF Camp A-341's area of operation to rise quickly. Friendly forces had to maneuver for best locations to attempt a river crossing, but it was still treacherous work.

After the Vietnamese soldier recovered enough to rejoin his unit, they found and booby-trapped a fishing net used by Viet Cong. A few minutes after leaving they heard the distant blast of the detonation.

The Soldier's Medal is awarded to any person of the Armed Forces of the United States or of a friendly foreign nation who while serving in any capacity with the Army of the United States distinguishes him/herself by heroism not involving actual conflict with an enemy. The performance must have involved personal hazard or danger and the voluntary risk of life under conditions not involving conflict with an armed enemy.

Chapter 15

1349 Backus Street, 1977

On January 13, after Grand Jury appearances by Lisbeth and Roger, detectives arrived at 1349 Backus. Sergeant Timmons, Detectives Omohundro, Brown, Reyes and Gomez, ID&R (Identification & Records) Officer Gurrola, Ranger Montemayor and ADA (Assistant District Attorney) Cowan interviewed Lisbeth, Roger and Lisbeth's brother Roger Gilman, and conducted a search of the premises.

The first thing detectives observed upon arrival was one half of the driveway was covered by dried milky white foam running from the closed garage to the street. Detectives looked at each other. *First things first*, they agreed. It was critical to obtain interviews from Lisbeth and Roger before upsetting them with an invasive search of the house. Consent to search could be rescinded at any time by Lisbeth or her attorney.

Detective Reginald Yearwood interviewed Roger, who essentially repeated what he had testified to, at the Grand Jury earlier that day regarding the events of January 3, and his and his mother's encounters with Jennifer Molina.

Roger also described another encounter with Molina. He said that in August 1976 he drove to his dad's BOQ to retrieve some baseball gear. He dropped his mother and brother off at a Fort Bliss bowling alley, drove to the BOQ, went in by himself with a key from his mother, and saw a woman sleeping in his dad's bed. They both asked who the other was. Roger did not remember what she said, but he identified himself as MAJ Garrett's son, retrieved the baseball equipment and left. Roger drove from the BOQ to LTC Hall's office and told him about the girl in his dad's bed. LTC Hall said he would talk to his father about it. Roger drove to the bowling alley and watched his mom and brother finish their game. He told his mother about the girl later that day, so his brother wouldn't overhear. His mother was disturbed at the news and said she would talk to Chester about it. About two weeks later when Roger was riding with his father in the Volkswagen, they spoke about the incident, and Chester apologized to Roger.

Regarding the baseball game incident, Roger said Chester asked Lisbeth to stop by his BOQ and pick up some socks he needed to play a baseball game. Lisbeth, Roger and Patrick went into the BOQ and saw the same girl sitting on the floor, watching television and smoking. Roger went into the other room to get Chester's socks and a couple of cassette tapes so he didn't know what the two women said, but when he came out he heard his mother ask the girl if she wanted to go to the baseball game, and she replied, "Yes, I'd like that very much." They all left together.

Chester was surprised to see the two ladies sitting together. Afterwards, Chester, Lisbeth and the woman talked while Roger and Patrick played on the field. The boys walked within earshot to hear Chester say, "I want to take my family to Italy." Lisbeth and the boys took the woman to her car at the BOQ and dropped her off. When they got home Chester was there. There was no argument but there was serious conversation between Chester and Lisbeth, and Chester spent the night. Roger stated his mother never assaulted or argued with the woman, and Roger didn't know of any time when his mother threatened this woman with a gun.

Roger closed the interview by saying he played basketball with his dad on New Year's Eve, and he had stopped by for a few minutes on New Year's Day.

Meanwhile, Detective John Omohundro interviewed Lisbeth in the presence of her attorney Michael Cohen. Lisbeth's statements matched her testimony at Grand Jury, but she added more detail. She stated she was 37 years old, had been married to Chester Garrett since 1963, and had lived at 1349 Backus since 1971. She said Chester returned from Thailand in October 1973 and lived at both 1349 Backus and at the BOQ.

Lisbeth said the last time she saw her husband was on January 3. They had some friends coming through town, Colonel and Mrs. Comee, on January 6. Chester came by the house to discuss plans for that visit. He arrived about 7:45pm, parked his Volkswagen in the driveway, and came into the house. Roger wanted to "shoot baskets" so he moved the Volkswagen into the garage. Chester and Lisbeth sat in the family room and discussed the Comees' visit. Chester left about 8:15pm or 8:20pm. Lisbeth and Roger were out front when he left. Patrick wasn't home; he had gone to a movie at Cielo Vista Mall. Roger went over to Robert Snelson's house to work on a term paper after Chester left. Patrick walked home and got there just before 10:00pm, and Roger arrived a few minutes later. Patrick went to bed while Roger went to the Snelson's house about 10:30pm, returning about 12:15am. Lisbeth didn't feel well and didn't do anything that night.

Lisbeth said she learned of Chester's death the next day from LTC Harrell Hall.

Lisbeth said she had filed for divorce about a year earlier, mainly to get Chester's attention and to get him "to get it together". She repeated the story about Chester's baseball game, stating that she, Roger and Patrick found a girl, PFC Molina, in Chester's room. Lisbeth simply asked her to go with them to the ball game and let Chester explain what she was doing in his BOQ. They took PFC Molina to the game and sat together. After the game Chester walked over to them, and Lisbeth told him she found PFC Molina in his room and that he needed to straighten out his life. Chester asked her to take Molina back, so she and the boys drove Molina to her car at

Fort Bliss and never saw her again.

Lisbeth said she didn't recall the last time Roger had driven the Volkswagen.

Lisbeth ended the interview stating she and Chester were getting their lives straightened out, were not having any problems, that she did not know who killed her husband, and she did not have any involvement in his death.

Between 2:30pm and 4:30pm, detectives scoured the house for clues. Detective Jesus Reyes took custody of several items of evidence from other detectives. Officers observed what appeared to be blood on the south wall of the garage, and Detective Reyes cut out a section of the stained drywall. Altogether, they collected 20 pieces of evidence in a short time, including soil samples, a gallon jug of Muriatic Acid, two pairs of tennis shoes, bucket and mop, broom, brushes, carpet, shirt, rag, residue samples and a tire iron.

Between 4:30pm and 5:00pm, Detective John Omohundro used a flashlight to inspect the walls and furniture in the kitchen. Lisbeth, her attorney Michael Cohen, and ADA John Cowan were in conversation in the kitchen and adjacent hallway. Detective Omohundro looked under the kitchen table and saw blood spatter on the wall behind the table. He reached out and felt small bumps of dried blood and inspected closer with his flashlight. It looked and felt like runs of dried red paint. Omohundro called Sergeant Timmons over.

Lisbeth saw where they were looking and starting yelling, "Stop! Stop! Get out! Get out!" Lisbeth's attorney Michael Cohen immediately revoked consent to search and ordered the detectives and ADA Cowan out of the house. Stunned detectives gathered evidence already taken and walked outside. ADA Cowan conferred with Attorney Cohen for a few moments and drove away without speaking to the detectives.

The detectives grouped by their vehicles and discussed what to do. Sergeant Timmons advised that, consent or no consent, they had enough evidence to secure a search warrant. Sergeant Timmons would go to the District Attorney's Office and secure one. The detectives left and drove to the Sheriff's office to wait for the warrant.

A search warrant was never obtained.

Chapter 16

Army Commendation Medal with V/Device
Vietnamese Gallantry Cross with Gold Star

On January 14, 1967, Captain Garrett was Special Forces Advisor to a Vietnamese force on a search and destroy mission in Phouc Long Province. One of the smaller field units became surrounded by a Viet Cong battalion. CPT Garrett immediately organized a reaction force and flew to the contact area by helicopter. Although his aircraft was the target of constant hostile fire, CPT Garrett coordinated air strikes against the Viet Cong elements and orbited the conflict for 40 minutes while the besieged unit prepared a landing zone. CPT Garrett then landed into live fire, deployed the reaction force, returned to base camp and returned with more reinforcements. CPT Garrett led the unit and reinforcements on a sweep through the entire combat area, killing 16 Viet Cong and gathering materials of valuable intelligence.

In a congratulatory teletype from the Lieutenant General/Deputy Commander of MACV (Military Assistance Command, Vietnam) to General Westmoreland, handwritten notes declared a total body count from CPT Garrett's encounter at 58, plus an additional 161 dead enemy from accompanying air strikes.

CPT Garrett was awarded the Army Commendation Medal with V/Device and the Republic of Vietnam Gallantry Cross with Gold Star for his actions that day.

The Army Commendation Medal is awarded to any member of the Armed Forces of the United States other than General Officers who, while serving in any capacity with the Army after 6 December 1941, distinguished himself by heroism, meritorious achievement or meritorious service. Awards may be made for acts of valor performed under circumstances described above which are of lesser degree than required for award of the Bronze Star Medal or for acts of noncombatant-related heroism which do not meet the requirements for an award of the Soldier's Medal.

The Republic of Vietnam Gallantry Cross was awarded to military personnel, civilians, and Armed Forces units and organizations in recognition of deeds of valor or heroic conduct while in combat with the enemy. The Republic of Vietnam Gallantry Cross was awarded in four degrees, with a basic medal followed by higher degrees which were the equivalent of personal citations on an organizational level. The degrees of the Gallantry Cross are as follows:

Gallantry Cross with Palm cited at the Armed Forces level.
Gallantry Cross with Gold Star cited at the Corps level.
Gallantry Cross with Silver Star cited at the Division level.
Gallantry Cross with Bronze Star cited at the Regiment level.

Chapter 17

On January 14, 1977, EPSD Sergeant Fred Timmons and Detective Wallace Brown briefed Army CID Special Agent Jack Hall and MAJ David McNeill, and advised them that EPSD's primary suspects were Lisbeth Garrett and her two sons, based on unidentified evidence and Lisbeth's "complete uncooperativeness." Time of death was estimated to be between 9:00pm and midnight on January 3, while cause of death was a blow to the back of the head by a blunt instrument. The stabbing injuries were inflicted after the head wound. Telephone records confirmed Chester Garrett was on his BOQ house phone between 8:30pm and 8:45pm, while Lisbeth claimed Garrett had been at their house around 8:15pm.

Also on January 14 Reverend Phillip Berry met with EPSD Detective H.Y. Gomez and gave him a handwritten letter from his teenage daughter Elaine Berry, who was acquainted with the Garrett family. Reverend Berry explained that his daughter knew the Garretts from living in the same neighborhood and her association with the Garrett brothers. Elaine Berry wrote the letter, an open letter to law enforcement, on January 11, 1977 after hearing of MAJ Garrett's death. The letter is as follows:

"Dear Sir,
"I just learned from my parents about the murder of Major Garrett which took place last week. I don't know whether you have any further information or not; from my own personal experiences, however, I feel that his family should not be put too far out of the picture. They can be a very deceiving group of people if they have reason to be.

"I have been a fairly close friend of the family for several years, and never have I seen such hatred and contempt as these people showed toward this man. During the holidays the bitterness seemed worse than ever. When I would question this attitude, I was told that it all stemmed from something that happened years ago and that I could never possibly understand. When I asked whether they couldn't just forgive the man and start over, the person always repeated that I just wouldn't understand. It was really strange.

"Roger Garrett, the oldest son, was known to talk openly with his friends about violence towards his father.

"I don't know whether you are aware of it already or not, but Mr. Garrett didn't live at home. He was not allowed in the house without an invitation. Once in a while he was allowed to come home for a trial basis to see whether he could "behave", but not for too long. Never more than two weeks to my knowledge. When he was there he was always wearing his warm-up suit. The family owned a dog; so if he had been home that day, which as I said before was unusual, he would probably have had dog hair on his warm-ups.

"This may not mean anything either; but for all the time I knew Mrs. Garrett, she has been very strict about alcohol. It was not tolerated by her or her husband. Around Thanksgiving time though, she had begun drinking seriously, and she encouraged her oldest son and his friends to drink too.

"All I can say is that Mr. Garrett was too big and cautious to let anyone else sneak up on him. At home he was completely different. They had taken away his spirit. The last time I saw him, he seemed to be at his emotions' end. No matter what they said or did to him, he took it. Maybe that counts for the lack of a struggle.

"Robert Snelson is a name I would look at closely, too. He is very close to Roger and Mrs. Garrett. He is a senior at either Burges or Eastwood High School. He is a bit on the unstable side.

"I don't know whether any of this has any significance or not, but if it can help in any way it was worth writing."

"Elaine Berry"

Also on January 14, FBI Special Agent Kenneth Cooper called EPSD Sergeant Fred Timmons and advised the anonymous caller who telephoned FBI Assistant Special Agent in Charge Thomas Westfall about Chester Garrett on January 7 and 10 was now identified as Garrett E. Hall of 10073 Imperial Drive, El Paso, Texas. SA Cooper also said Hall's information that Chester Garrett was killed by drug dealers was unreliable and not valid but did not elaborate further.

On January 18, Detective John Omohundro interviewed Roger's friend Robert Snelson, age seventeen. Robert Snelson said he had known Roger for more than five years and they were best friends. They played sports together and sometimes played basketball with MAJ Garrett. He knew MAJ and Mrs. Garrett had filed for divorce and the Major lived on post, but Roger never gave him details and Robert never asked.

Robert said Roger told him the family was going to Italy soon and knew Roger was excited about going to Europe and going to school there.

Robert said January 3 was the first day of school after Christmas break, but Robert stayed home sick. He said Roger came to his house about 11:00am to help him with a school paper and stayed until 3:00pm. Roger came back to Robert's house sometime between 8:00pm and 9:00pm. Roger told Robert he took his brother somewhere and asked Robert to call Roger's house around 10:00pm. Robert noticed Roger was driving his mom's Mercury.

At 10:00pm Robert called Roger's house. Lisbeth answered and told Robert that Roger had left to pick up Patrick, and she would have Roger call him when he returned. Roger did call Robert between 10:15pm and 10:30pm and asked Robert to come to Roger's house to work on his school paper. Robert asked his father, who said Robert couldn't leave but Roger could come to the Snelson house if he wanted. Roger arrived a few minutes later and stayed until about 12:30am.

The next day Robert went to school. After school, about 4:00pm, he called Roger, who "sounded down." Robert asked Roger what the matter was, and "he said his father was dead." Roger couldn't go into details or talk too long as he was concerned about his mother.

While Detective Omohundro was interviewing Robert

Snelson, Sergeant Fred Timmons interviewed Robert's father, Harry Snelson. Mr. Snelson knew of the Garrett family through his son Robert for five years or more. He only met MAJ Garrett one time, approximately 18 months before, when MAJ Garrett came to the Snelson house looking for Roger, who wasn't there. Later Mr. Snelson learned Roger was actually in the house then, sleeping in Robert's closet. It angered Mr. Snelson that he had inadvertently lied to MAJ Garrett. Mr. Snelson confirmed that Roger was a frequent visitor to the Snelson home.

Harry Snelson said that on January 3, his son Robert stayed home as he wasn't feeling well. Toward evening Robert felt well enough to do homework and telephone friends. A short time after 10:00pm, Robert came to him and asked if he could go over to Roger's house to do homework. Harry said no; Robert couldn't leave but Roger could come to their house if he wanted. Harry Snelson recalled Roger came to the Snelson house at about 11:15pm. Harry went to bed at midnight, but checked on Robert twice and thought Roger stayed "a couple of hours."

On January 21, Detective Reyes sent 61 pieces of evidence, including suspected blood samples from the Garrett home, to the FBI laboratory in Quantico, Virginia, for analysis.

On January 27, LTC Harrell Hall applied for a posthumous Legion of Merit award for MAJ Chester Garrett. On January 31, LTC Hall received a memo from Colonel Russell McGraw, Commanding Officer of the Fort Bliss Air Defense Artillery, downgrading LTC Hall's request for a Legion of Merit award to a Meritorious Service Award. In late February Hall received another memo from McGraw confirming Garrett's Meritorious Service Award.

On March 16, 1977, the FBI Identification Division, Latent Fingerprint Section, sent a report to El Paso County Sheriff Mike Sullivan and Captain Mac Stout. The report referenced items from Chester Garrett's Volkswagen submitted by Detective Jesus Reyes, and advised that eleven latent fingerprints and three latent palm prints were recovered. Some were identified as Chester Garrett's prints, others were not identified, and none belonged to Lisbeth or Roger Garrett.

A separate FBI Laboratory report detailed results of blood and hair samples submitted by Detective Reyes. Some blood samples were grouped as Type "O", several samples were identified as human origin but insufficient in quantity as to determine blood type, and others were not blood at all. Hair samples were identified only by color and as "Caucasian origin."

On April 13, 1977, the Veterans Administration sent a letter to the EPPD Chief of Police referencing a "claim of benefits" by Lisbeth Garrett and requested to know if Lisbeth was a suspect in MAJ Garrett's murder investigation. This letter set off a chain of correspondence lasting until December 1977. EPPD must have replied claiming no knowledge of the murder, as the next letter from the Veterans Administration to EPPD, dated May 2, reads as follows:

> "In reference to your note of 4-22-77, you will find a copy of the death certificate attached. As you can see, it was a homicide and the body was found on the Avenue of the Americas. Perhaps this will help in your search for information. You must have a record of a violent death inside the city limits."

EPPD in turn must have contacted EPSD as the next piece of correspondence discovered was from EPSD to the Veterans Administration on May 6, and reads:

> "TO WHOM IT MAY CONCERN
> "Reference your request on the above captioned, this letter is to advise you that our case is still presently under investigation and will remain so until the case can be closed by arrest. We are unable to say at this time if the claimant was involved or not as our investigation is still continuing."

On May 19, the Veterans Administration responded:

> "Thank you for your prompt answer. We must not only determine the degree of involvement on the part of the claimants, but the issue of misconduct on the part of the veteran. Please keep us informed, as the claim will be held in pending status until we can make

our legal decisions based on the evidence you will submit to us."

The "pending status" of the Veterans Administration benefits claim must have worn thin on Lisbeth, because on December 20 her attorney Larry Schwartz wrote Sheriff Mike Sullivan:

"In the past I have attempted to get clarified the status of the Garrett case. We have been contacted by the Veterans Administration and advised that they could not resolve the benefits for the Garrett children and Mrs. Garrett until the Sheriff's Department in El Paso, Texas, advised them that they were no longer pursuing any charges against the Garretts. We have been advised verbally that this was the case; however, apparently no one in the Sheriff's Department was authorized to write such a letter at the time…The delay in receiving benefits is working a great hardship on the Garretts and quite frankly, I believe an injustice on them, and we would appreciate your clearing this up as soon as possible."

Sheriff Mike Sullivan's response on December 27:

"In reference to your letter dated December 20, 1977, concerning the estate of Major Chester Garrett, I regret to inform you that your request will not be complied with at this time. The investigation surrounding the death of Major Garrett is very active, and this department has hopes of solving the matter. However, we do not know how long it will take. Until it is resolved, any notification to the Veterans Administration by this office is impossible."

Chapter 18

1975 Ft. Bliss Falcons basketball team

While EPSD's investigation proceeded with Lisbeth and/or Roger as primary suspects, the Federal Bureau of Investigation and Army Criminal Investigation Division shifted their focus towards the black soldiers, PFC Eugene Thomas and SP4 Howard Jackson, who were cut from the basketball team on the day Garrett was killed.

A former soldier named Donald Smith was a main instigator of the FBI's and Army CID's renewed interest in the basketball players. Smith's "cooperation" was initiated by his wife, who lived in New York City and contacted the FBI office there, stating her husband told her he had observed the death of MAJ Garrett on January 3, 1977 at a gymnasium at Fort Bliss. One subject was alleged to own a late 60s Cadillac, white over green, silver tinted windows and whitewall tires. This description exactly matched Eugene Thomas' vehicle. Since Thomas was an original suspect from the first day, Smith's information was certainly relevant.

On May 17, 1977, FBI SA Gary Webb told EPSD Sergeant Fred Timmons someone named Loretta Smith in New York City contacted New York Housing Police and advised that her husband Donald Smith and two GIs beat an army captain to death and dumped his body at Fort Bliss about four months before. This was the first time Donald Smith appeared on any radar regarding Chester Garrett's death. Donald Smith was a soldier who eventually provided a worm-hole portal for investigators into several areas of criminal activity conducted by soldiers in Texas, California, New York, Korea and Germany.

This short, slender, soft spoken young man intrigued federal investigators and prosecutors with stories of drug trafficking, theft, sexual perversions, extortion, blackmail, kidnapping and prostitution. Some of it was even true. The most significant aspect of Donald Smith's wriggling under the federal microscope, though, was his ability to derail a relatively straight-forward murder investigation, one that local investigators already solved but lacked evidence to prosecute, and cause the federal government to spend thousands of man hours and untold amounts of money on results as meaningful as a wisp of smoke. The entire saga was initiated by a domestic dispute between husband and wife in the projects of New York City.

On May 18, 1977, the day after FBI SA Webb told Sergeant Timmons about Donald Smith in El Paso, two agents from FBI New York, SAs Daniel Lyons and John Kunst, interviewed New York City Housing Authority Patrolmen William Phillips and Alan Lennox.

Patrolman William Phillips said he and Patrolman Clarence Shannon responded to a domestic dispute on May 13 on Clinton Street in Brooklyn at the residence of Donald and Loretta Smith. Donald Smith accused Loretta Smith of stabbing him. The couple was transported to a police station, where Loretta said her husband was wanted in Fort Bliss, El Paso, Texas for murdering a U.S. Army Captain. Patrolman Phillips said Donald Smith's demeanor and attitude changed immediately. Donald Smith stated he no longer wanted to press charges. At this point Phillips was going off duty, and the interview was handed over to Patrolman Lennox. Phillips knew Donald Smith was later taken to a hospital where he received seven stitches for a stab wound in his back.

Patrolman Alan Lennox said he interviewed Donald and Loretta Smith during May 13 and 14. Loretta Smith told Patrolman Lennox that Donald told her he might be wanted in connection with a homicide of an army captain at Fort Bliss, El Paso, Texas, about four months before. She said her husband Donald was discharged from the army but two other men involved were still soldiers. Loretta told Patrolman Lennox the men supposedly beat the Captain to death and threw his body out in Fort Bliss.

FBI Agents Lyons and Kunst interviewed Loretta Smith the same day, who said while she had no direct knowledge of a murder of an army officer at Fort Bliss, Texas, her husband Donald Smith told her several times he had been implicated in such a murder, along with a black soldier named Jerry Bland. Loretta said her husband and Bland, and a person named "Fresno", played in a band and lived together at 1700 Keltner Avenue, El Paso, Texas.

Loretta Smith said her husband returned to New York from El Paso three months before, telling her it was getting too "hot" for him there. Donald Smith told Loretta he was implicated in the murder, although he had nothing to do with it. Loretta gave the FBI agents the names of Sergeant and Mrs. Lawrence Cooley of Fort Bliss as possibly having more information.

Loretta Smith added that Jerry Bland had implicated her husband in a theft of a government typewriter from Fort Bliss, currently stored at 1700 Keltner in El Paso.

The FBI interviews with Loretta Smith and Housing Authority Patrolmen in New York triggered a flurry of activity in El Paso and at Fort Bliss. The following day FBI SA Gary Webb and EPSD Sergeant Fred Timmons met and researched available records on Donald Smith, Fresnel Sorel, Lawrence Cooley and Jerry Bland.

On May 20 SA Gary Webb and Sergeant Fred Timmons interviewed Staff Sergeant Larry Cooley at Fort Bliss CID. SSG Cooley stated he did not know anyone named Donald or Loretta Smith and he has never received phone calls from New York. He said he had been stationed at Fort Bliss since October 1973. Cooley said he did not personally know MAJ Garrett but knew he was assigned to A Battery, Headquarters Command. Cooley was shown a photograph of Donald Smith. Cooley was initially unable to identify the photograph but after a few minutes said, "I do know this man and his wife."

Cooley explained he and his former wife were managers of Sarador Apartments near Dyer Street from late 1974 until early 1975. They were friends with a couple named Gil and Dianne McKinley, and thought they met Donald and Loretta Smith through the McKinleys. Cooley said he had not seen the Smiths since he and his ex-wife quit the apartment manager job in May or June 1975. Cooley told investigators the McKinleys and Smiths smoked marijuana, and he and his ex-wife joined them numerous times to do so in the McKinleys' apartment.

On May 25, SSG Cooley was interviewed again at Army CID by FBI SA Webb, Sergeant Timmons and Detective Jesus Reyes. Cooley advised he had spoken to his ex-wife since the previous interview and could confirm he had never spoken to Loretta Smith by telephone, certainly not since January 1977, and definitely not about the death of MAJ Garrett. He also confirmed with his ex-wife that neither one of them had spoken to or seen Loretta or Donald Smith since 1975 when they quit being apartment managers.

SSG Cooley said he remembered McKinley told him Loretta Smith ordered Donald Smith around and was obviously the boss. Cooley concluded the interview by saying he did not remember ever meeting MAJ Garrett personally, probably because he was not athletically inclined, didn't play basketball and did not hang out at the gymnasiums at Fort Bliss.

On May 27, Sergeant Timmons, Detective Reyes and FBI SA Webb interviewed Specialist-4 Theodore (Jerry) Bland at Army CID. SP4 Bland stated he knew MAJ Chester Garrett through the basketball team. MAJ Garrett helped him join the team when Bland arrived at Fort Bliss in October or November 1974. SP4 Bland said he knew Donald Smith well, since they worked together at Fort Bliss until Donald Smith left for New York some five or six months before. Bland said he met Donald's wife Loretta but didn't know her very well. He had little to do with her but knew she was dominant in her relationship with Donald.

SP4 Bland said Donald Smith was the basketball team trainer and statistician, and that Smith and MAJ Garrett got along well. Bland claimed no knowledge that Donald Smith was ever considered a suspect in Garrett's murder.

Bland advised even though he and Donald Smith were friends and co-workers, he found Smith to be very effeminate, and several people suspected Smith was gay. Bland said Smith compensated for poor athleticism and girlish manners by being extremely intelligent.

Bland said he also knew "Fresnel." Bland knew he was a

student at the El Paso Community College and that he lived in an apartment on Keltner Street. Donald Smith often stayed there with Fresnel.

SP4 Bland said Donald Smith and Fresnel were in a band called "Opodium Starship". Fresnel played lead guitar, and Donald Smith was the manager and sound man.

SP4 Bland said Donald Smith didn't act like a "tough guy," nor was he a tough guy. Bland thought if Smith was mad enough to kill someone, he suspected Smith would waylay the person. Bland also said he suspected basketball players Thomas and Jackson of killing MAJ Garrett since they argued with MAJ Garrett before his body was found. Bland said that on May 26, the day before, while on a bus with Eugene Thomas returning home from New Mexico, Thomas said Jackson intended to be a starter on the team next year, and might be able to do so since he "wouldn't have to kill anyone this year."

SP4 Bland said he had seen Donald Smith smoke marijuana and said it made Smith very "flakey." He remembered once when Smith attacked his girlfriend, Dia, while under the influence of marijuana and wine. Bland had to pull Smith off of Dia because he was choking her in a state of rage. Dia told Bland one time that Smith was "into something real big" that could get them both in a lot of trouble.

Chapter 19

After Garrett's first deployment to Vietnam, he arrived to his next assignment at Fort Bragg, North Carolina. He served as a Company Commander, Basic Combat Training Brigade, U.S. Army Training Center Infantry. Garrett matched his high expectations. He produced the most Outstanding Company in the brigade for three consecutive training cycles between May 1967 and April 1968. His company was awarded an "Excellent" rating during the Annual General Inspection. The company's consistently low AWOL rate and exceptional high morale among his cadre and trainees was attributed to his outstanding leadership ability. In addition to full time dedication to his company, Garrett attended University of Nebraska at Omaha to complete his Baccalaureate Degree. He attended from April 1968 to March 1969 and earned a Business Administration degree in May 1969.

Garrett's OER from spring of 1968 speaks volumes. His Battalion Commander wrote:

> "Captain Garrett is an extremely competent officer and has produced outstanding results. During the last four training cycles he produced the outstanding company in the battalion and for the last two cycles his company was honored as the outstanding company in the brigade. I consider CPT Garrett to be an outstanding officer."

The Brigade Commander wrote:

> "Captain Garrett is the strongest company commander I have known in my military experience and the most outstanding unit commander in this 25 company brigade. He is a very strong willed officer and a fierce competitor. At times he lacked patience and tact in dealing with supporting agencies and superiors.

Nevertheless, his performance has been truly outstanding. His company easily led the brigade in overall training and set a training record in PT."

    Garrett completed the Infantry Officer Advance Course in January 1970. Garrett continued his professional military development by attending U.S. Army Ranger Course # 9-70. Garrett was recognized as Distinguished Graduate and was awarded the coveted Darby Award at completion of the Ranger Course in March 1970. The Darby Award goes to the graduate who shows the best tactical and administrative leadership performance, attains the most positive "spot" reports, and demonstrates being a cut above the rest. The Darby Award is named in honor of Brigadier General William O. Darby, who organized the 1st Ranger Battalion in 1942 with handpicked volunteers leading the way onto the beaches of North Africa.

Chapter 20

On June 21, 1977, Specialist-4 Jennifer Molina was interviewed by FBI SA Gary Webb, Army CID SA J.W. Gee, MPI (Military Police Inspector) SGT Elmo Boggs, EPSD Sergeant Fred Timmons and Detective H.Y. Gomez at Fort Bliss CID.

Army CID Special Agent James "J.W." Gee was not new to the army but new to Army CID, just out of the CID academy. Six feet tall, 180 pounds, short military haircut and mustache, his peers teased that he looked like a young Omar Sharif. J.W. threw himself into the Garrett investigation and became well known to the EPSD detectives. Later interviews with SA J.W. Gee indicate he was keenly interested in solving the murder and frustrated by Army CID's "rules of engagement" that prohibit CID from investigating anything without nexus to the U.S. Army. While "nexus" could be a gray area that might allow proactive investigative operations with the thinnest threads of military connection, CID management seemed far more conservative, perhaps to avoid any criticism for perceived interference in investigations outside its jurisdiction. This conservative policy has caused frustration for many CID investigators who are eager to solve and clear cases. While SA Gee had been in frequent contact with EPSD detectives since January, this interview was his first recorded participation in the Garrett investigation.

SP4 Molina was presented a photograph of Donald Smith, whom she said she did not know by name or photo. The name Jerry Bland was familiar, but she could not say why. The name Fresnel Sorel was not familiar, nor did she know anyone named Thomas.

SP4 Molina did know Roosevelt Hill, though. She said he was a cook in the dining facility where she ate. He asked Molina out when she was new, and she told him "to get lost." After that he was usually mean and vulgar to her.

With reference to her initial interviews on January 5 and 6, Jennifer Molina advised the reason she had her friend Charles Hicks drive her past MAJ Garrett's BOQ at about 11:45pm on January 3 upon her return to El Paso after annual leave was to determine whether Garrett was home. Molina said she was definitely jealous of MAJ Garrett and his wife. She said while she did not return to the BOQ that night, she did check other places on post where he could have gone.

Molina advised since MAJ Garrett's death she had received several "weird" telephone calls in which the caller would not speak. She said the calls stopped about one month prior.

Jennifer Molina said MAJ Garrett did not drink, smoke or swear in front of her. He was vain about his appearance and an immaculate dresser. Molina said MAJ Garrett was a "god" in his battalion and a god in his home. She said MAJ Garrett told her his goals were to become a general, and in the far future the President of the United States, and he was not joking. He told Molina he went into the Army because in the Marine Corps he would never get beyond rank of Major, and he did not go Air Force because he could not qualify for flight status. She said he constantly told her that, as a Major, he could do whatever he wanted in the Army.

SP4 Molina said MAJ Garrett would not take any drugs and was reluctant to even take motion sickness pills.

Jennifer Molina said "Chet" told her he married his wife at age seventeen and she was two years older than he. He was trying out for the Chicago Cubs baseball team in Arizona at the time. His wife became pregnant and went home to Dallas to have the baby. Chester told Molina his mother-in-law, whom he despised, talked his wife out of returning to him in Arizona (it's unknown how Molina came by this false history). While MAJ Garrett was in Vietnam his mother-in-law was mugged in Dallas and died as a result. His wife wanted him to return for the funeral but Garrett refused. Shortly after, Garrett received Rest & Recreation leave and planned to travel to Dallas to see his family, but Lisbeth sent word through an Air Force Chaplain that he was not to come home. Garrett spent his R&R in Saigon instead. On his next R&R, Lisbeth agreed to meet him in Hawaii, but when he arrived he learned she had brought the children with her and was not interested in spending time with him.

Molina said her intimate relationship with Garrett began the night of February 6, 1976. She had gone to his office at Student Battalion to complain that people were saying she was transferred from School Battalion because she was "shacking up" with him. She arrived at his office at about 4:30pm, as they spoke the mood went from official to intimate, and they had sex. She left his office about 9:00pm and went to her barracks. About an hour later he called her and invited her to his BOQ, where they continued sexual relations until about 4am. Molina said after that night they were constantly together until December 1976. Jennifer Molina said their relationship was primarily based on sex, although it was serious enough that she introduced MAJ Garrett to her father and sister when they visited El Paso in June 1976.

SP4 Molina said she first met Mrs. Garrett in July 1976, when Mrs. Garrett surprised her in MAJ Garrett's bed at the BOQ. Molina said Mrs. Garrett beat her with a steam iron and a belt until she passed out.

Molina said Mrs. Garrett caught her in the BOQ again in August 1976. She asked Molina if she would accompany her to MAJ Garrett's baseball game and advised if Molina declined she would shoot Molina with a P-38 pistol. Molina agreed to go. They went to the ball game where Chester was playing. He saw them, came over, and Lisbeth asked him if he wanted to marry "Miss Molina" or if he wanted to go home to his family. Chester Garrett said he would go home with Mrs. Garrett. A few days later MAJ Garrett called Jennifer Molina to his BOQ and they resumed their previous relationship.

Molina said she did not know if MAJ Garrett was dating any other women, although she heard about a woman who worked in the dining facility. She said she would have been jealous but would not have "raised a fuss", and simply waited her turn with him.

Jennifer Molina said she went home on annual leave in December 1976, for two weeks, returning on the night of January 3. Her friend Charlie Hicks picked her up, drove her past MAJ Garrett's BOQ, and to her barracks where she signed in coming off annual leave. They returned to the airport to retrieve her luggage, went out for a meal and a few drinks, and she returned to her room about 2:30am. She woke at 5:30am and had breakfast with Charlie Hicks.

SP4 Molina concluded the interview by stating she did not kill MAJ Garrett but suspected his wife killed him, because during one of their encounters Mrs. Garrett told her if she wanted MAJ Garrett, "all she would get was a corpse."

Chapter 21

Chester Garrett proceeded on his second tour in Vietnam in March 1970. He was assigned to Headquarters, Headquarters Company (HHC), 1st Battalion, 12th Infantry, 4th Infantry Division as the Battalion Operations Officer. Garrett made such a positive impact to the Battalion's combat operations that a special Officer Evaluation Report on his performance was written after four and a half months into the assignment. The admiration of Garrett's chain-of-command was obvious.

His battalion commander wrote:

> "MAJ Garrett has been assigned to this battalion for only a short time. This officer, as the battalion operations officer, is so exceptionally outstanding in this capacity that a special report was considered appropriate. He possesses a keen intellect and a depth in understanding the nature of jungle combat operations that mark him as a primary asset to this battalion. MAJ Garrett is a true professional soldier who molds stern discipline with the optimum degree of compassion and concern for his subordinates. He has displayed a deep feeling for the private soldier and his proficiency in combat. This officer's vast store of experience in jungle combat operations enabled him to increase the combat effectiveness of this battalion in a short period. He is truly an outstanding officer in all respects and of great future potential to the U.S. Army. He should be seriously considered for promotion ahead of his contemporaries and for advanced civil and military schooling."

Garrett's brigade commander endorsed the same OER:

> "Major Garrett has performed in an

outstanding manner. Aggressive, frank, and completely dedicated. An officer of highest principles and standards. Outstanding qualities of leadership. He works with great enthusiasm and possesses an inquisitive mind. He strives for perfection—a top flight officer."

In August 1970, Garrett was transferred to the 2nd Battalion, 35th Infantry as the Battalion S-3. The battalion commander wanted a strong leader in that position, and Garrett's thorough understanding of jungle combat operations was a primary asset. The battalion commander issued the following OER:

"MAJ Garrett is the most outstanding battalion operations officer that I have known. His detailed knowledge of tactics and techniques contributed immeasurably to the successful accomplishment of the Battalion mission. It is largely due to his ability to organize, plan, issue detailed guidance, and supervise that this battalion became well known for its excellent combat assaults. Besides being the battalion operations officer he also acted as the executive officer for the battalion forward element. MAJ Garrett prides himself on his professionalism and establishes high end and exacting standards for himself and his subordinates. Recommend that he be considered for acceptance for advanced civil schooling."

Garrett's brigade commander endorsed the OER:

"I transferred Major Garrett to become the S-3, 2nd Battalion 35th Infantry because the battalion needed strength in that position. Major Garrett provided just that and there was an immediate improvement noted in the operational and training procedures."

From December 1970 through March 1971, Garrett was

assigned to HHC, 3rd Brigade, 101st Airborne Division, (Airmobile) in Vietnam. He was assigned as Base Defense Officer for Camp Evans and provided expert guidance and supervision to six sector commanders of the Camp Evans perimeter line.

Garrett was reassigned on March 17, 1971, to assume duties of combat Infantry Battalion S-3. During combat operations in March 1971, the commander and S-3 for 3rd Battalion (Airmobile), 187th Infantry, 101st Airborne Division (Airmobile) were killed in a helicopter crash. They were replaced by Colonel Robert Stevenson and CPT Garrett. Garrett was wounded and awarded the Purple Heart, 2nd Oak Leaf Cluster, during Operation Lam Son 719/Dewey Canyon II.

Garrett's OER for March through May 1971, acknowledged his strong infantry attributes but also contained a reprimand for temper and tact issues. His battalion commander wrote:

> "Major Garrett is one of the most intense officers I have ever known. He approaches each task or situation with intensity and stubbornness that is found in very few officers. He is a highly proficient infantry field soldier and has a good grasp of infantry airmobile concepts and tactics in the counterinsurgency environment. On occasion his quick temper and lack of tact resulted in less than superior performance. If Major Garrett overcomes his temper and tact problems, he will be a definite asset to the Army in higher staff positions."

His brigade commander endorsed the OER:

> "Major Garrett has the potential of becoming an outstanding Infantry officer. He knows tactics and is extraordinarily endowed with courage and physical ability. Major Garrett possesses a dynamic personality and exudes ambition and drive. This get-on-with-it outlook tends to make him impatient and curt with superior and subordinate alike. Major Garrett must control this tendency in order to become the outstanding officer he can so readily be. I recommend that he attend the Command and General Staff College early in his career.

The exposure to varying opinions and outlooks of his peers may be the influence that enables him to erase this one small blemish in his overall make up. I would readily accept Major Garrett again in any operational environment."

Chapter 22

On June 22, investigators interviewed Military Police SP4 Paul Belvin, PFC Jonathan Brewington, SP4 Jerry Bland, Fresnel Sorel and Annitta Bell.

SP4 Paul Belvin was an MP who witnessed the January 3 argument between MAJ Garrett, PFC Eugene Thomas and SP4 Howard Jackson, but he was unable to provide any actionable information.

PFC Jonathan Brewington was a drummer for Opodium Starship and had known Donald Smith through the band since August 1976. Brewington was a classmate of Jennifer Molina's in AIT. He knew Molina was dating MAJ Garrett and even drove his car sometimes. Brewington confirmed that Jennifer Molina and Donald Smith did not know each other. He also said he knew Donald Smith smoked marijuana but claimed no knowledge of Smith trafficking drugs or stolen items.

SP4 Jerry Bland said Fresnel Sorel told him MAJ Garrett was dating a female Specialist-4 who drove a white Mark IV Continental, but he didn't know her or her name. Bland said Donald Smith told him he owed money to some rough people, and that Fresnel should "look out" because these bad people knew Fresnel and Donald were friends. Fresnel Sorel told Jerry Bland that Donald's wife kept calling his apartment looking for Donald and asking for money. Fresnel also told Jerry Bland that Donald Smith owed Fresnel $150, that Fresnel confronted Donald at El Paso International Airport when Donald tried to skip town, and Donald had threatened Fresnel.

FBI SA Gary Webb and EPSD Sergeant Fred Timmons went to Fresnel Sorel's apartment on Keltner Street and interviewed him. Fresnel Sorel told them he met Donald Smith in December 1976, through Jerry Bland, and Smith moved in with him and became manager and equipment man for his band, Opodium Starship. Sorel said Donald Smith received a grant of $1,000 to attend El Paso Community College, but Smith used the money to travel home to New York instead. Sorel said he loaned Smith $195 but Smith wouldn't pay him back. Sorel tracked Smith to El Paso International

Airport as Smith was about to leave for New York and confronted him. Smith agreed to accompany Sorel to the apartment. Donald Smith told Fresnel Sorel two men were looking for him, the same men who had murdered MAJ Garrett, and they meant to do harm to Smith. Smith said they beat Garrett to death, stabbed him, drove him out into the desert and dumped his body. Smith told Sorel those men were going to cut off Sorel's left hand just because Sorel was his friend. Smith told Sorel that Garrett's death was tied to a stolen typewriter and the basketball team. Sorel noted that Donald Smith did not say Roderick Gathright was one of the murderers but that Gathright was present when Garrett was killed.

SA Webb and Sgt Timmons left Fresnel Sorel and located Annitta Bell, sister of Dia Willis, who was Donald Smith's girlfriend and a close friend of Jerry Bland. Annitta advised that Dia was currently living in Los Angeles. Annitta Bell described "Smitty" (Donald Smith) as a thief who stole a piano or electric organ from Holloman Air Force Base (AFB) in New Mexico during a band gig. Once he came home with a very powerful and expensive vacuum cleaner, also from Holloman AFB. He also stole other things like ashtrays and once stole several typewriters. He stored stolen goods at Dia's apartment in El Paso. She recounted Smith's misuse of the $1,000 school grant. Annitta advised that Donald Smith was "heavy into marijuana" and was selling "lids" (ounces of marijuana) from his apartment on Keltner. She said the whole band, Opodium Starship, was involved; they pooled their money to buy large amounts of marijuana which they resold and split profits.

On June 23, Investigators Webb, Gee, Boggs, Timmons and Gomez met and compared notes. FBI SA Gary Webb stated PFC Eugene Thomas and SP4 Howard Jackson may have killed MAJ Garrett based on information received from a witness named Donald Smith.

Investigators and detectives of any agency are compelled to follow any lead regardless of how ridiculous it may appear at the time. Any possible lead to solving crime, in this case a particularly brutal murder of a high ranking, highly decorated military officer, had to be checked out. For example, the anonymous calls to the FBI claiming MAJ Garrett was extorting drug dealers were quickly ruled out but still had to be researched, as did Donald Smith's truths, half-truths and lies.

Chapter 23

In summer of 1977, the investigation continued but with a pronounced limp. Donald Smith had implied to FBI New York that PFC Roderick Gathright was a direct witness to Garrett's murder by PFC Eugene Thomas and SP4 Howard Jackson. Gathright was already known to Army CID and FBI as a suspect facing federal prosecution for numerous accounts of theft of government property. MPI (Military Police Inspector) SGT Boggs had an informant who kept tabs on various soldiers of interest. This informant told Boggs that Gathright was staying with Eugene Thomas and confirmed Thomas' known address.

On the evening of June 23 investigators banged on Eugene Thomas' door; he agreed to go with them to be interviewed at Fort Bliss CID. FBI SA Webb, Army CID SA Gee, EPSD Sergeant Timmons, EPSD Detective Gomez and Army SGT Boggs discussed with Eugene Thomas his actions on January 3. Thomas again described the confrontation he and Howard Jackson had with MAJ Garrett at the gym when he cut them from the team. Thomas detailed how he drove Jackson to his home and then with his friend David Smith coordinated a double date with two girls, Irma Leal and "Birdie", resulting in an all-nighter at the Howard Johnson's Motel. The next morning Thomas and Smith went to work and learned of MAJ Garrett's death.

Investigators shifted to Eugene Thomas' knowledge of Roderick Gathright, also a basketball team player, and as it turned out, a distant cousin also from Thomas' home town of Louisville, Kentucky. When asked about his knowledge of Gathright's involvement in the theft of an electric typewriter from their unit's headquarters, Thomas said he overheard an argument between Gathright and another basketball teammate, Jerry Bland. Bland was on duty at HQS when Gathright allegedly stole the typewriter and Bland was initially blamed. Gathright denied he was involved in the theft, but Bland still blamed Gathright for getting him in trouble.

Eugene Thomas identified Donald Smith from a photograph,

saying he met him once at an apartment on Keltner Street. He said he did not know anyone named Fresnel Sorel or Roosevelt Hill. Thomas ended the interview by stating he had no knowledge or involvement in the death of MAJ Garrett.

Investigators interviewed SP4 James Barber, Eugene Thomas' barracks roommate, who confirmed Thomas' alibi for January 3 as far as his coming and going to the barracks and the gym. Barber also saw Thomas and David Smith in the barracks parking lot that afternoon with two women. Barber denied any knowledge of MAJ Garrett's death. He said he knew Roderick Gathright in passing and provided details of the last few times he had seen Gathright.

They interviewed SP5 David Smith, who verified Thomas' statements regarding the evening of January 3 with the two girls at the Howard Johnson's Motel.

On June 24, 1977, the same five investigators interviewed SP4 Howard Jackson at Army CID on Fort Bliss. SP4 Jackson said he had been manager of the basketball team since October 1976. MAJ Chester Garrett was assistant coach during Jackson's entire association with the team. On January 3 MAJ Garrett cut Howard Jackson and Eugene Thomas because they missed too many practices during the December holidays. Jackson said he did argue with MAJ Garrett, but he wasn't so mad at him as to do him physical harm. Jackson described Chester Garrett as "hard core" military, by the book, tough but fair, and had never hurt him prior to that date. Jackson repeated the same details of his whereabouts on the night of January 3 has he told them in his first interview on January 4; Eugene Thomas gave him a ride to his home on Magruder Street, and he stayed home that night with his wife and baby. Two friends stopped to visit for 30-45 minutes around 8:00pm. He went to work as usual the next morning and didn't hear of MAJ Garrett's death until that night when Army CID agents approached him after his Battery Commander called him back to work.

SP4 Howard Jackson said all he knew about MAJ Garrett outside of basketball was that he drove a red Volkswagen Beetle. Jackson knew Donald Smith and Jerry Bland through basketball, and felt it likely that MAJ Garrett and Donald Smith knew each other since Smith was the team trainer before Jackson, and Smith finished his army tour in July 1976.

Howard Jackson said he knew Donald Smith was a heavy marijuana smoker, but he never knew Smith to sell marijuana, and he had no knowledge of Smith being involved in theft on or off Fort Bliss.

Howard Jackson said he did know Roderick Gathright as a basketball teammate, and he knew that Gathright and Jerry Bland, another player, didn't get along over a typewriter being stolen from 11th group Headquarters while Bland was assigned there as a duty driver. Bland accused Gathright of stealing it. Jackson stated no knowledge of any problems between MAJ Garrett and Gathright, and he didn't recall ever seeing Gathright or Thomas hanging out with Donald Smith. Jackson also said he no knowledge of MAJ Garrett having a girlfriend, never heard of Jennifer Molina, and knew nothing about stolen vacuum cleaners, pianos or televisions.

On June 27, FBI SA Webb, MPI SGT Boggs, Sheriff's Sergeant Timmons and Detective Gomez interviewed Fresnel Sorel in his apartment on Keltner Street. Sorel said he formed a band, Opodium Starship, in August 1976. Fresnel Sorel said he met Donald Smith through a friend, Curtis Austin. Donald Smith introduced Fresnel Sorel to Jerry Bland. Smith and Bland lived together for six or seven months, until Bland bought a car and couldn't afford to live off post anymore, so Donald Smith moved in with Fresnel Sorel on Keltner Street.

Fresnel Sorel said Donald Smith went back to his wife in New York City in March 1977, but not before he stiffed Sorel for rent plus a $195 loan. Donald Smith spent his last three nights with a woman named Pam Wilson. Sorel went to Pam's apartment to collect the $195 and on arrival saw Smith loading suitcases into a taxi. Smith told Sorel he left the money he owed Sorel with Pam to pay Sorel. Sorel went to Pam's apartment where she told him she had no idea what Sorel was talking about. Sorel ran down to the parking lot in time to see Smith's taxi driving away. Sorel chased the taxi to the airport and confronted Smith. Smith, who had missed his flight anyway, agreed to go with Sorel to his apartment on Keltner.

At the apartment Donald Smith told Fresnel Sorel two guys were after him. Smith said a month before these two unnamed men snatched Smith and took him to a house where there were a lot of guns and knives, told Smith he knew too much, and they were going to "cut his ass up" unless he gave them some money. They also said they knew Smith was friends with Sorel, and were going to cut off Sorel's left hand and "mess him up good."

Donald Smith told Fresnel Sorel the two men were "Jeff" and "Eddie", and Eddie was on the basketball team, from Kentucky and drove a green Cadillac. Smith told Sorel that Jeff, Eddie and Roderick Gathright were involved in killing MAJ Garrett. Smith said Jeff and Eddie "knocked Major Garrett on the head", stabbed him 37 times, put him in the back seat of his Volkswagen, drove him off Fort Bliss, and dumped him and the car out near McCombs and Dyer Streets in the desert. Smith told Sorel he had seen Jeff and Eddie with Gathright many times.

Fresnel Sorel said that one time before Gathright was transferred to Germany, Gathright arrived at Sorel's and Donald Smith's apartment with a large electric IBM typewriter, which Sorel assumed was stolen. Sorel sold the typewriter a few days later for eighty dollars and gave the money to Gathright. Sorel told the investigators he thought he knew where the typewriter currently was, and he could attempt to retrieve it.

Fresnel Sorel told the investigators Donald Smith did in fact steal an electric organ, but not from Alamogordo, New Mexico. Sorel said Smith took the organ from the Hilton Inn by El Paso International Airport, which Sorel personally returned so his band could play there in the future.

On the same date, FBI SA Gary Webb and Army CID SGT Elmo Boggs located and interviewed Private Roosevelt Hill at his apartment on Truman Street. PVT Hill said he knew MAJ Chester Garrett because the Major routinely ate at the mess hall where Hill was a cook. Hill said he never had problems with MAJ Garrett, and was surprised to learn the Major filed charges that caused him to be put in the brig. Hill felt certain it was in retaliation for Hill making comments to MAJ Garrett's girlfriend, Jennifer Molina, about dating her and about her "social activities." Hill explained he didn't know positively that Molina was dating MAJ Garrett, but that was one rumor among many rumors that Molina dated "everyone in sight", that MAJ Garrett transferred Molina out of the Student Battalion and under MAJ Garrett's command for romantic reasons, and that she was generally promiscuous. Hill didn't like Molina because she was a "smart aleck woman" who put him down and caused him embarrassment on numerous occasions.

PVT Hill said he did not kill MAJ Garrett nor did he have anyone else kill MAJ Garrett. Hill advised he was good at karate and skilled with "Numchuk" fighting sticks, and would fight anyone, but he would not fight to the point of killing anyone.

On the same day, SAs Gary Webb and J.W. Gee interviewed Jerry Bland at Army CID on Fort Bliss. Jerry Bland said that on the day the typewriter was stolen he was assigned as Duty Driver at Group Headquarters and he loaned his car keys to a soldier named Roberts. Those keys also included a key to the Duty Officer's Building. Bland and the Duty Officer left on an errand, and when he returned he found his keys laying on the desk in the "duty shack." He was assigned as Duty Driver the entire night and was released the next morning. Upon arriving at his barracks to get some sleep he was ordered to return to the duty shack, where he was questioned by MPs about a missing typewriter from the duty shack. He did not tell the MPs about loaning his keys to Roberts, but when he was released he hunted Roberts down, who told Bland he had given the keys to Roderick Gathright to return the keys to Bland.

Jerry Bland said he tracked down Gathright, who told Bland he had taken the typewriter, and gave it to Donald Smith to sell. Bland went to Donald Smith's apartment on Keltner Street and found the typewriter. Bland said he tried to get Smith and Gathright to return the typewriter, but they wouldn't, and Bland was afraid to take it himself because Gathright and Smith would hurt him. Bland knew they sold the typewriter, but they were unsure to whom.

On June 28, 1977, FBI Special Agents Rodney Davis and John Kunst interviewed Donald Smith in Brooklyn, New York. Smith said he had been stationed in the Army at Fort Bliss, and after he was discharged he stayed a few more months in El Paso, Texas. His full stay in El Paso was from September 1974 until January 1977 when he returned to New York. Smith said he was a trainer for the Fort Bliss Basketball Team and, as such, he got to know MAJ Chester Garrett who was an assistant coach. Donald Smith told the agents he learned of MAJ Garrett's death from the local paper after he was discharged from the army and that was all he knew about Garrett's death. Smith said he never told his wife he was connected in any way to Garrett's murder. Smith said he withdrew his complaint against his wife after she stabbed him in the Red Hook Housing Project because she was the mother of his two children and someone had to take care of them.

Donald Smith said his girlfriend "Dia" (Ardular Graham) knew MAJ Garrett only in that she was a cheerleader for the basketball team, and did not know him personally. Smith said he moved in with Fresnel Sorel at 3700 Keltner Street after he was discharged from the Army, but Smith never told Sorel he had any knowledge of the Garrett murder.

Donald Smith said he knew Jerry Bland, Roderick Gathright and members of the band Opodium Starship, but he denied knowing anyone who belonged to a theft ring or was involved in the sale of marijuana in El Paso. Smith professed to not using any drugs himself, including marijuana or alcohol. He also said he was not afraid of anyone in El Paso and nobody was out to kill him because he was a witness to the Garrett murder.

Donald Smith ended the interview by stating he had nothing to do with MAJ Garrett's death. While FBI interviewed Donald Smith in New York, FBI also interviewed Ardular Willis nee Graham in Los Angeles. SAs Jerry Delap and Joseph Varley met her on West 73rd Street. Ardular Willis said she was introduced to Donald Smith in April 1976 through Jerry Bland. Although Willis was involved in a common law relationship with her now-husband Bernard Willis, Bernard had transferred to Germany, and Ardular started dating Donald Smith and allowed him to move in with her for a few days at a time. Ardular Willis advised their relationship lasted until Christmas 1976.

Willis said Donald Smith was a trainer on the Fort Bliss basketball team; she used to attend the games and met several players and MAJ Garrett, whom she recalled as a "nice guy." She said Donald Smith was discharged in July 1976, and he spent his time at her apartment or at the apartment of Fresnel Sorel, who had a band called Opodium Starship. Donald Smith became the equipment manager of the band, and Willis accompanied him on a couple of gigs. Willis said Donald Smith used the band's appearances as an opportunity to steal from the clubs they played at. During a gig at Holloman AFB in New Mexico, Smith stole a large commercial type vacuum cleaner. On New Year's Eve 1976, Donald Smith stole a keyboard and an amplifier from the Waldo Pepper Club in El Paso. Once she visited Fresnel Sorel's apartment and saw an electric IBM typewriter. Willis was certain the typewriter was government property because she had been employed as a typist on similar typewriters for the government in the past.

Ardular Willis said she and Donald Smith got into a heated argument over the future of their relationship on Christmas Eve 1976. Smith wanted to maintain a casual non-involved relationship while Willis wanted a serious and profound understanding between them. They argued until Donald Smith assaulted Ardular Willis and performed a "sexual perversion" on her person. Willis refused to detail what Smith did to her, but she said when Smith tried to strangle her she was saved from death by Jerry Bland, who jumped on Donald Smith and pulled him off of her. Ardular Willis intended to file charges against him but never did. Four days later Donald Smith called Ardular, apologized and asked her out to a New Year's Eve party, which she accepted, but she knew their relationship was over.

Ardular Willis said Donald Smith was in her apartment on January 4 or 5 when they heard on broadcast news that MAJ Garrett had been killed. Donald Smith said "what a trip," when they heard the news, and she never heard him speak of it ever again. Donald Smith departed El Paso about three weeks later, promising to return soon to El Paso, but she never heard from him again.

Ardular Willis summed up Donald Smith as a "lazy shiftless alcoholic who would do almost anything for money." He smoked marijuana and occasionally sold it, but to her knowledge was not involved with hard drugs.

On June 29, 1977, Army CID SA J.W. Gee contacted Chief Warrant Officer (CW4) Ray Kangus, a Homicide Instructor at the U.S. Army Military Police School in Fort McClellen, Alabama, and described the manner in which MAJ Garrett had been killed. After some discussion regarding the width and depth of the stab wounds, CW4 Kangus concluded the stabber was probably a woman.

That afternoon, Army CID SA J.W. Gee and FBI SA Gary Webb interviewed Erlinda Juarez, a civilian dining hall worker at Fort Bliss. Miss Juarez repeated what she had told EPSD Detective Wallace Brown in January; she had known MAJ Garrett since early 1975, he helped her son, a former soldier, with some problems concerning an AWOL charge that affected his discharge. Afterwards Ms Juarez and MAJ Garrett became romantically involved and saw each other about twice a month at his BOQ room. Her last social contact with MAJ Garrett was on Christmas Eve when she went to his BOQ and he gave her a Christmas present. The final time Ms Juarez saw him was at the dining facility at about 8am on January, the day of his death. She said he seemed disturbed and distracted at that time.

Ms Juarez said she did not know of MAJ Garrett's relationship with his wife but had heard rumors in the dining facility he had a relationship with a female soldier, Jennifer Molina. Juarez knew Molina because she ate in the mess hall two or three times a week. Ms Juarez said the idea of MAJ Garrett dating Molina did not bother her. Ms Juarez stated no knowledge of who might have killed MAJ Garrett.

On the morning of June 30, Army CID SA J.W. Gee reviewed the Sheriff's Office case file and came across the reports regarding the anonymous telephone calls to FBI El Paso that MAJ Garrett was involved in a drug ring in El Paso. SA Gee found the allegations ludicrous, but he saw the name Edward Courtois mentioned. Remembering Fresnel Sorel reported that Donald Smith blamed Garrett's murder on "Ed and Jeff", he wondered at a connection between "Ed" and Edward Courtois. SA Gee's research found Courtois had been transferred to the 31st Infantry in Korea. SA Gee placed a call to Courtois' unit and spoke to Sergeant First Class Raymond McDonald. SFC McDonald told SA Gee that Staff Sergeant Edward Courtois was a problem child in the unit and unable to perform to the standards of his rank in any assigned position, so was currently assigned to permanent CQ (Charge of Quarters) duty. SFC McDonald knew SSG Courtois and his wife Katherine had been charged with child abuse and negligence in El Paso.

SA J.W. Gee contacted Abby Jones of the Department of Welfare in El Paso. Mrs. Jones said she was familiar with the Courtois family and the court case. Mrs. Jones was unable to officially comment upon the court case but could relate personal information about Edward and Katherine Courtois. Abby Jones said they were both "junkies", and Katherine's parents, Garnett and Agnes Hall, filed a child abuse case against them to obtain custody of their children. Mrs. Jones said Katherine was an open lesbian and her partner lived with her and Edward. Edward and Katherine both had violent tempers, examples of which were substantiated in court.

The Halls won custody of the children, but Mr. Garnett Hall died of a heart attack shortly after. Garnett Hall was likely the anonymous caller to the FBI shortly after the murder, later identified by them as "Garrett Hall."

SA J.W. Gee contacted Mrs. Agnes Hall via telephone. Mrs. Hall verified she had custody of both children, and described Katherine and Edward Courtois as narcotics users and dealers with violent tempers. Mrs. Hall said they were always six or seven months behind in their bills and habitually short of even enough money to feed themselves.

Chapter 24

Distinguished Flying Cross

On July 23, 1970, MAJ Chester Garrett, serving as S-3 Operations Officer of 1st Battalion, 12th Infantry, 4th Infantry Division, was conducting an aerial reconnaissance flight and detected an estimated company-size enemy force. As Major Garrett maintained surveillance of the enemy force, 12th Infantry units were combat assaulted into the enemy area. As gunships were called in for support, Major Garrett commanded his aircraft to drop smoke grenades to identify the friendly forces for the gunships. Even while heavy enemy fire ricocheted through his aircraft, Major Garrett held his position and continued to coordinate the ground assault and place fire upon the enemy positions. Major Garrett's effective direction of ground forces, artillery and gunships accounted for 32 enemy soldiers killed during the operation.

Major Garrett was awarded the Distinguished Flying Cross for his actions that day. It is unusual for an individual that is neither a pilot nor air crew to be awarded a Distinguished Flying Cross. Major Garrett was acting only in a temporary capacity as an air observer.

The Distinguished Flying Cross is awarded to any person who, while serving in any capacity with the Armed Forces of the United States, distinguishes himself by heroism or extraordinary achievement while participating in aerial flight. The performance of the act of heroism must be evidenced by voluntary action above and beyond the call of duty. The extraordinary achievement must have resulted in an accomplishment so exceptional and outstanding as to clearly set the individual apart from his comrades or from other persons in similar circumstances.

Chapter 25

Early on July 1, Army CID SA J.W. Gee and FBI SA Gary Webb interviewed LTC Harrell Hall again about Chester Garrett. LTC Hall described Garrett as a highly respected and highly decorated soldier, who was "held in awe" by his peers due to his Vietnam war hero status. LTC Hall said MAJ Garrett was aggressive but fair in dealing with other people, and a bit of a crusader when it came to helping enlisted soldiers with their personal or professional problems. LTC Hall was aware of MAJ Garrett's marital issues and had met Lisbeth Garrett several times. LTC Hall was also aware of MAJ Garrett's romantic involvements with other women at Fort Bliss and with 1st Lieutenant Karen McClellan, daughter of MAJ General Stan Leon McClellan, currently assigned to Fort Meade, Maryland. LTC Hall was under the impression MAJ Garrett planned to marry 1LT McClellan.

LTC Hall again noted some of MAJ Garrett's career high points. LTC Hall stated that Garrett once played professional baseball with a minor league club of the Chicago Cubs; originally joined the Army as an enlisted man in the 101st Airborne; selected as Division Soldier of the Year; went to the West Point Prep school but didn't graduate to attend West Point as he was married. He also said Garrett was commissioned in 1963 and went through Ranger School as a Captain. LTC Hall mentioned MAJ Garrett's three tours in Vietnam, and that he had been at Fort Bliss about three and a half years. MAJ Garrett inspired confidence due to his self-confidence gained from field and training experience. LTC Hall said MAJ Garrett was one of the few men LTC Hall would want with him in a tough or nasty situation.

LTC Hall said MAJ Garrett was known to be a lady's man and to have numerous affairs. He said the only affair that caused him embarrassment was his most recent one with the enlisted soldier Jennifer Molina. LTC Hall felt MAJ Garrett's real problem was his wife and sons. Lisbeth Garrett had thrown Chester Garrett out of their home in late 1974 or early 1975 and filed for divorce, but refused to sign the final decree, holding it over his head "like a guillotine." MAJ Garrett had brought Lisbeth to dinner at the Hall home one time, and both Colonel and Mrs. Hall agreed Mrs. Garrett was "a little off in the head." LTC Hall said he did not know the origin of Chester and Lisbeth Garrett's problems as Chester refused to discuss it. LTC Hall said Lisbeth completely won over her sons and used them to spy on MAJ Garrett. She once said she had to show the boys "the type of animal the Major was." LTC Hall said Lisbeth called him several times and came to his office once to complain about their problems, and his oldest son Roger came to his office once about MAJ Garrett having a girl in his BOQ.

Lisbeth called LTC Hall one time and said she could put MAJ Garrett in prison because he had taken their jointly-owned stock and tried to cash it after coercing Ann Echols, a former secretary, to forge Lisbeth's signature on the stock. Lisbeth advised LTC Hall she later gained Ann Echols' confidence and employed her as a spy on Chester Garrett.

Later Roger found Jennifer Molina at the Major's BOQ. Roger went directly to LTC Hall's office and reported it, stating his family could use the incident to get more money from MAJ Garrett, or at least use it to hurt him.

LTC Hall said that in about June 1976, Mrs. Garrett came to his office and reported Chester Garrett was a bad person who brutalized her and her sons, and that the Major was seeing other women. She said she forced him out of her house but would not let him go even though she despised him. LTC Hall said Lisbeth "just could not seem to rationalize that Major Garrett could be free to see other women."

LTC Hall closed the interview by advising he could not eliminate the Garrett family as prime suspects, or at least conspirators, in the death of Chester Garrett as they had everything to gain financially due to his death and everything to lose if he divorced Mrs. Garrett.

Chapter 26

After their interview with LTC Hall, SAs Gee and Webb contacted Ruth Smith nee Hall, Katherine Courtois' sister, in El Paso about her knowledge of Edward and Katherine Courtois. Ruth Smith said the Courtoises were involved with a band called Opodium Starship. Smith described the Courtoises as "junkies" who used cocaine and amphetamines, and were involved in a swinger's club organized by a Reverend Wally Chapman. Ruth Smith said Chapman seemed to live well but had no "visible means of support."

Ruth Smith said both Courtoises had bad tempers and Edward Courtois threatened Smith several times due to her testimony against the Courtoises during the child custody suit. Ruth Smith stated one time when he threatened her life, Edward Courtois stated, "I can get anyone in this town snuffed for fifty dollars. It would be no problem."

Ruth Smith also said Edward Courtois was stealing government equipment. She said he stored stolen items; tools, army cots, bedding, etc. at her apartment until spring of 1976, which she demanded he move out. While Ruth Smith felt Edward Courtois was capable of killing someone, she had no knowledge of who killed MAJ Garrett.

At 3:00pm that afternoon, SA J.W. Gee received a call from PFC Eugene Thomas, who said he heard that a girl he dated once, Verline Wilson, said she knew who killed MAJ Garrett. SA Gee went to Verline Wilson's home on Taxco Street in El Paso and spoke to her. Verline said she had no firsthand knowledge of MAJ Garrett's death, but a friend of hers, Donna McCarthy, said a guy named "Rod" killed Garrett.

On the same day, July 1, FBI SA Claude Martin interviewed U.S. Army CPT Gregory Laskow, Ph.D., in San Antonio, Texas. CPT Laskow stated he had been stationed at William Beaumont Army Hospital at Fort Bliss and had treated both MAJ Chester Garrett and his wife, Lisbeth Garrett. CPT Laskow said Garrett's marital problems were due in part to MAJ Garrett's high personal standards and disappointment that Lisbeth constantly contradicted him regarding discipline for his two sons. CPT Laskow said MAJ Garrett was of large physical stature and in excellent physical condition and wanted his children to be excellent athletes as well. CPT Laskow considered MAJ Garrett to be opinionated and intimidating in dealing with people. CPT Laskow noted MAJ Garrett voluntarily terminated treatment with Laskow and did not see him again.

Chapter 27

On July 6, Army CID Special Agent J.W. Gee interviewed Specialist 5 Joseph Hammond, who worked in Student Battalion Headquarters with MAJ Chester Garrett. SP5 Hammond said he met MAJ Garrett in March 1975 and maintained daily professional contact with him until January 3, 1977. Hammond described MAJ Garrett as "professional, hardcore, but fair", and very loyal to subordinates. He had a reputation as a problem solver for enlisted personnel. SP5 Hammond was aware MAJ Garrett was dating SP4 Jennifer Molina, as Molina called MAJ Garrett at the office about three times a week. Hammond learned to recognize Molina's voice even though she identified herself as "Mrs. Charles."

SP5 Hammond told SA Gee the only person he thought might have a reason to kill MAJ Garrett was Roosevelt Hill, who had been a cook in a dining facility MAJ Garrett was in charge of. Hammond said MAJ Garrett was responsible for getting Hill a Bad Conduct Discharge from the Army due to Hill's repeated arrests by El Paso Police for aggravated assault, concealed weapons and illegal drugs.

Special Agent J.W. Gee interviewed CPT Stephen Orrison, who met MAJ Garrett in April 1976, and had regular professional and social contact with Garrett until his death. CPT Orrison described MAJ Garrett as a highly decorated professional soldier with a reputation as a problem solver, especially with young enlisted troops who frequently came to him with problems. CPT Orrison said he was aware the Major and his wife were having marital problems and were legally separated. CPT Orrison had been around MAJ Garrett's eldest son Roger on several occasions, and felt it obvious Roger did not like his father. MAJ Garrett was aware of Roger's ill will and made efforts to improve their relationship. For example, MAJ Garrett coached Roger's baseball team to ensure Roger got a lot of playing time, and MAJ Garrett made arrangements to secure a baseball scholarship to attend Texas A&M University, which Roger declined after Mrs. Garrett "voiced her dissatisfaction."

CPT Orrison recalled a remark MAJ Garrett made in late December 1976 after a particularly heated argument with Mrs. Garrett over the phone. The Major said, "She thinks she's going to Naples with me. That's a crock of shit. They're not going." CPT Orrison gathered that Mrs. Garrett did not like MAJ Garrett or the military.

CPT Orrison said, after MAJ Garrett's death, he was responsible for itemizing and documenting MAJ Garrett's personal effects from his office and BOQ room, during which he came across several letters from a Lieutenant Karen McClellan. From their content, CPT Orrison surmised MAJ Garrett met Lieutenant McClellan in Vietnam, and there were remarks pertaining to marriage between them. In her final letter, McClellan said she would not seriously consider a relationship with MAJ Garrett until he sorted out his domestic issues with Mrs. Garrett.

After speaking with CPT Orrison, SA J.W. Gee contacted MAJ John Whitehouse, who was appointed as Lisbeth's Survival Assistance Officer. MAJ Whitehouse said he had met MAJ Garrett once or twice but could not recall when. MAJ Whitehouse told SA Gee through his association with Mrs. Garrett and her two sons, he learned MAJ Garrett was an "aggressive, abrupt and abrasive person" who lost his temper easily. Lisbeth and Roger both told MAJ Whitehouse that MAJ Garrett beat them frequently, and Lisbeth was aware of affairs with at least two women.

MAJ Whitehouse said as a result of MAJ Garrett's death, Mrs. Garrett received a $3,000 death gratuity, any back pay owed MAJ Garrett, a $20,000 SGLI Insurance Policy, an initial $10,000 death gratuity plus a subsequent $2,000 death gratuity from Army Mutual Aid, life insurance payments from two civilian policies (amounts unknown), a social security death gratuity (amount unknown), and a monthly pension check from social security until the youngest child turned eighteen. Mrs. Garrett also received all of MAJ Garrett's property, including home, furniture and two vehicles. Mrs. Garrett had not yet received any assistance from the Veteran's Administration, but she was interested in obtaining assistance as Roger was planning on attending Texas A&M in the fall. Mrs. Garrett was also eligible to receive a VA death gratuity, and the boys were eligible to receive education assistance. However, the VA contacted EPSD and determined Mrs. Garrett was regarded as a potential suspect in MAJ Garrett's death. Until Mrs. Garrett was eliminated as a suspect, the VA would not release any benefits to her family.

On July 9, CID SA J.W. Gee took a sworn statement from Fresnel Sorel. Sorel said he met Donald Smith through a friend, Curtis Austin. Sorel knew Austin was gay, and Austin told Sorel that Donald Smith was one of his "tricks", implying Austin was sexually active with Smith. When Smith was discharged from the army, possibly in July 1976, he moved in with Sorel on Keltner Street and Smith's wife went home to New York. In August 1976, Sorel formed a musical band, Opodium Starship, and hired Donald Smith to be equipment manager.

Fresnel Sorel repeated the episode in which Donald Smith tried to skip town owing him back rent, how he chased Smith to the airport, and the story Smith told him about "Gene and Jeff" killing MAJ Garrett.

Referencing the stolen typewriter, Sorel said he knew Roderick Gathright stole a large IBM electric typewriter from some place where Jerry Bland was on duty. Sorel knew this because Donald Smith told him Gathright wanted to talk to Sorel about buying it. Sorel found a buyer, Sherine Dickson, who paid Gathright eighty dollars for it, while Sorel received nothing. He said Donald Smith told him that day at the airport the typewriter was tied somehow into MAJ Garrett's death. Sorel quoted Donald Smith as saying, "If the cops cannot find the typewriter, they would not be able to solve the murder." Sorel said Sherine Dickson and her soldier husband were transferred from Fort Bliss to Germany. She contacted Sorel and said she and her husband split up, she was on her way to California and her husband was shipping her stuff, including the typewriter, when she settled in California.

SA Gee reminded Sorel in his initial statement to FBI he called Donald Smith's would-be assassins "Ed and Jeff" and now he called them "Gene and Jeff". Sorel explained when he first heard of the threat he told his girlfriend, Tania Beasley, if anything happened to him these guys "Gene and Jeff" would likely be responsible. She wrote those names in her diary, and recently when he incorrectly referred to them as "Ed and Jeff" she corrected him with her diary.

Chapter 28

On July 11, Special Agent J.W. Gee interviewed Elaine Berry, the Garrett neighbor who wrote the open letter to law enforcement. Miss Berry said while she had known the Garrett family for about five years, she was most familiar with the oldest son Roger. She said Roger "hated his father" because he had done something for which they could never forgive him. Roger claimed his father had beaten him and his mother several times. Elaine Berry quoted Roger as saying if his father ever came near him or his mother again, he would use a baseball bat he had in the garage on him. Berry said she never saw that baseball bat and never saw MAJ Garrett strike Roger or Mrs. Garrett. Mrs. Garrett told Elaine Berry she did not love MAJ Garrett and would have divorced him if it were financially possible. Elaine said Mrs. Garrett was traditionally strictly opposed to alcohol but by fall of 1976, she was drinking heavily and often encouraged Elaine to drink with her, which she always declined.

Elaine Berry last saw MAJ Garrett during the Christmas holidays at the Garrett house. She said MAJ Garrett looked "extremely detached and depressed" as Mrs. Garrett and Roger viciously teased and swore at him. Elaine thought this very unusual as the Major normally did not tolerate cursing, yet there he sat without objection as they cursed him. Roger told Elaine, "We caught him again", and explained it was about another woman.

Elaine Berry said she had no knowledge as to who killed MAJ Garrett but felt it "extremely possible" Mrs. Garrett and Roger could have done it.

Chapter 29

Bronze Star, 3rd Oak Leaf Cluster

Major Garrett was awarded his 4th Bronze Star for "exceptionally meritorious achievement" before and during Operation LAMSON 71, March 1-22, 1971, in the Quang Tri Province. Operation LAMSON 71 was an invasion of southern Laos by South Vietnamese forces to disrupt communist supply and infiltration networks along Route 9 in that country. The operation was supported by U.S. airpower, and by U.S. artillery fire support from firebases inside South Vietnam. Major Garrett had recently assumed command of Fire Support Base Ann and found it in need of extensive repairs. In spite of a lack of physical resources, he led a security platoon in refurbishing the fire base and constructed an artillery "fighting hill" that delivered accurate protective fire for local population centers and assault positions in time for Operation LAMSON 71.

Chapter 30

On July 13, Army CID SA J.W. Gee interviewed Fresnel Sorel's girlfriend, Tania Beasley. Tania said she met Sorel in August 1976 and had maintained daily contact with him since. When they first met, Sorel was living in an apartment on Keltner with Donald Smith. Tania said Smith moved out on January 11, 1977, and she knew this because she made an entry in her diary. On January 21, Sorel called Tania and told her how Donald Smith tried to skip town without paying Sorel money he was owed and told Sorel about the guys "Gene and Jeff" who were going to hurt both Smith and Sorel. Sorel told her at the time to write those names in her diary in case anything bad happened to Sorel. Tania arrived at the interview with her diary and SA Gee made a copy of the diary entry that mentioned "Gene and Jeff."

On July 15, FBI Special Agent James Beck met PFC Eugene Thomas at Fort Bliss CID. Thomas gave consent for his apartment on Nike Lane to be searched, so the FBI performed a search and located nothing of interest other than several bizarre photos of dead bodies on display in Thomas' bedroom, which Thomas referred to as "conversation pieces."

On July 18, CID Special Agent J.W. Gee interviewed Staff Sergeant Bennett Reynolds, who worked with MAJ Garrett at School Battalion Headquarters. SSG Reynolds said he had daily professional contact with MAJ Garrett from July 1975 until his death. SSG Reynolds described MAJ Garrett as short tempered and impulsive. He was also a very aggressive problem solver, especially in dealing with enlisted soldiers' problems. SSG Reynolds never observed the Major being physical when he was angry, but in the summer of 1976, Mrs. Garrett came to the office and claimed MAJ Garrett had given her a black eye. SSG Reynolds knew MAJ Garrett was dating a female soldier who drove a Lincoln Continental Mark IV. SSG Reynolds was aware of Roosevelt Hill's issues with the Major but did not feel them to be a reason to kill MAJ Garrett.

After speaking to SSG Reynolds, SA Gee interviewed

Command Sergeant Major (CSM) Franklin Moses in the same office. CSM Moses said he had worked with MAJ Garrett on a daily basis from August 1976 until his death. CSM Moses described MAJ Garrett as a "soldier's soldier, very stern and not necessarily the type of person who would accept that something could not be done." He said MAJ Garrett was very aggressive and tended to be abrasive when trying to accomplish a task. In regard to the fact MAJ Garrett's BOQ room was found with lights on and a half-eaten sandwich left on the table, CSM Moses said MAJ Garrett was a voracious eater and would not leave food uneaten; rather, he would have taken the food with him. MAJ Garrett was also energy conscious and routinely turned off lights in any unoccupied offices he happened to pass, and it would be very unusual for the Major to leave lights on in his BOQ. CSM Moses knew MAJ Garrett was dating an enlisted female named Molina but had no knowledge of MAJ Garrett's relationship with family members.

On July 19, Army CID Special Agent J.W. Gee and FBI Special Agent James Beck interviewed Donna McCarthy. Miss McCarthy said she attended a party at a night club called "Mr. G" on Mesa Street in El Paso in January or February 1977. She was sitting with her girlfriend, Michelle King, who pointed out Roderick Gathright and said, "Rod stabbed him", in reference to MAJ Garrett's death. Miss McCarthy knew Gathright through the band Opodium Starship, and she knew Fresnel Sorel and Donald Smith the same way.

On the same day SAs James Beck and J. W. Gee conducted a consensual search of 1349 Backus, a few weeks after Lisbeth and the boys moved to Gallic Court. A green hatchet and a rubber truncheon were located in the garage, as well as reddish brown stains on the floor between the family room and kitchen. Similar stains were found on the interior garage door and door frame between the family room and kitchen. Scrapings of stains were taken as evidence, as well as the hatchet and truncheon.

On July 20, SA J.W. Gee interviewed Army Chaplain CPT David Farr, who said he met MAJ Garrett in November 1974, and kept regular contact with him until December 30, 1976, the last time they met. CPT Farr estimates he met Lisbeth perhaps six times in all. CPT Farr described MAJ Garrett as very professional and "probably the finest officer assigned to Fort Bliss." CPT Farr said Garrett was very confident of his abilities and aggressive in completing assignments. He had a volatile temper, but CPT Farr felt he would not strike anyone. CPT Farr thought MAJ Garrett's career was the single most important thing to him. CPT Farr knew Lisbeth openly opposed MAJ Garrett's harsh discipline in family matters and knew one time Lisbeth complained to LTC Harrell Hall that MAJ Garrett allegedly bashed Roger's head into a wall during an argument.

CPT Farr handled MAJ Garrett's funeral arrangements and found Lisbeth's reaction to MAJ Garrett's death and funeral "a bit peculiar". In his experience as a chaplain he found Lisbeth's manner to be "matter of fact" and with far less grief than other widows. CPT Farr described Roger's comportment to be identical to Lisbeth's, and in his opinion, neither Lisbeth nor Roger seemed surprised or excessively concerned about Chester Garrett's death.

Also on July 20, Doctor Vincent DiMaio of Southwestern Institute of Forensic Sciences in Dallas, Texas, sent a letter to CID Special Agent J.W. Gee. Also enclosed was a three page preliminary autopsy report and twenty color photographs of the deceased and his clothing. A portion of the letter reads as follows:

> "The first thing that strikes me about the case is the brutality of the assault on Major Garrett. He was struck multiple times about the head with great force and stabbed multiple times in the left side and back. Such an attack is usually inflicted during an acute episode of rage. I would think it unlikely that the assailant is a female, due to the savage nature of the attack. However, I would not be at all surprised to find out that a female is involved, possibly as an accomplice or maybe as a motive for the attack.
>
> "In view of the distribution of the injuries, I think the assault on Major Garrett was in two stages. First, I believe, he was struck about the head with a heavy object, probably having some irregularities to its surface. During part of the attack, the Major was conscious and tried to ward off the blows. This is shown by the bruise and abrasions to the back of the right hand.

"I think that, after being severely beaten about the head, Major Garrett then pitched forward, probably landing on the right side of his face. There are two injuries on the right side of his face, one involving the right side of his chin and the other just below the right eyebrow. The injury to the chin is described by the prosecutor as a stab wound. It does not, however, go into the mouth and I think possibly that this is not truly a stab wound, but a laceration. This wound and the wound of the eye could possibly be due to a blunt injury, i.e. being struck by the weapon used to inflict the head injuries or possibly due to the deceased's impacting on the ground with the right side of his face.

"I believe the second stage of the attack occurred after Major Garrett collapsed to the ground, This was the multiple stab wounds of the left side and left back. I think it is significant that the wounds, with only one exception, were all on the left side and back. If the Major was up and moving about in a struggle, one would expect the wounds to be distributed more evenly over the body. If, however, he was face down on the ground, someone could very easily squat down or kneel down beside the body and inflict all these wounds. In my opinion, the Major was alive at the time he was stabbed. Survival following the head injuries and stab wounds was probably short; less than one hour.

"Following death, the Major's body was then apparently placed in the backseat of a Volkswagen. I would think it extremely unlikely, almost impossible, for an average-sized woman to have manipulated the body of the deceased into the backseat of a Volkswagen. It is possible for one man to do this, but I would think it would be more likely for two individuals, one at least a man, to have accomplished this feat. I think it is of note that the body was placed in the backseat of the car.

If there was only one individual driving the car and only one individual involved, why not place the body in the right front-seat, rather than in the back?"

On July 21, Army CID Special Agent Jackie Wilson interviewed Lieutenant Colonel William Comee in Hawaii. LTC Comee and MAJ Garrett were neighbors and co-students while assigned to Fort Benning, Georgia in 1969. LTC Comee described MAJ Garrett as a huge, physically strong person, very emotional and confrontational, which LTC Comee believed contributed to the Major's marital problems. LTC Comee said MAJ Garrett would get upset over little things that normally would not bother a person, especially where his family was concerned.

LTC William Comee said in 1972, when the Garrett family was stationed at Fort Bragg, North Carolina, Lisbeth contemplated divorce, as Chester Garrett would apparently strike her when angry. However, when he completed his third tour in Vietnam and was assigned to Fort Bliss, he and Lisbeth agreed they would stay together if he would seek psychiatric treatment for his emotional problems. Later LTC Comee learned MAJ Garrett separated from his family and lived on post in BOQ, and was apparently involved with a female officer. LTC Comee clarified he had no firsthand knowledge nor had he witnessed any incidents between MAJ Garrett and his wife, but MAJ Garrett had told him several times he had caused his wife and family a lot of pain and heartache.

LTC Comee said the last time he spoke with MAJ Garrett was during November 1976, when Garrett told him his marriage problems were resolved; he had orders to Italy and his family was going to accompany him. In the same conversation LTC Comee informed MAJ Garrett he had orders to Hawaii, and he and his wife planned to stop and visit the Garrett family while en route. Upon their arrival in El Paso in January 1977, they learned of Chester Garrett's death.

Chapter 31

On July 25, Army CID SA Gee and FBI SA Beck interviewed Chester Garrett's sister, Cheryl Smith. Cheryl said while she lived in El Paso she had only limited contact with her brother, although she felt they were close. She said she saw Chester and a girlfriend, Sharon Turner, at a restaurant three or four weeks before he was killed. Cheryl said Chester seemed happy with Sharon Turner, and Chester described Sharon to Cheryl as very religious and unaware Chester was married. Cheryl said Chester's marriage was extremely difficult. Her belief was Lisbeth never loved Chester and they never really got along. Cheryl described Lisbeth as a constant complainer and as extravagant. Money was a constant dispute between them, as Chester was thrifty and tried to save money.

Cheryl Smith emphasized that Lisbeth was obsessed with money and felt money was the reason Lisbeth didn't sign the divorce papers. Cheryl also heard from Lisbeth that just prior to his death Chester took out a $100,000 life insurance policy with Lisbeth as the beneficiary.

Cheryl Smith said Chester Garrett's numerous affairs were also a constant source of dispute with Lisbeth. Cheryl told the agents that after the murder, his girlfriend Sharon Turner told her Chester had promised to marry her and take her to Italy on his impending transfer. Sharon Turner was so certain of marriage she had picked out a wedding dress.

Cheryl Smith also mentioned a former coworker, Bettie Montoya, who knew Chester from her job as manager of the Officers' Club. Cheryl said Chester had an affair with Bettie Montoya, who told Cheryl Smith she was in love with Chester and threatened suicide when she heard of Chester's death.

After speaking with Cheryl Smith, SA J.W. Gee went to the Officers' Club and found Bettie Montoya. Bettie said she first met Chester Garrett in summer 1975 and last saw him on January 3, the day he was killed, at about 4pm. Bettie Montoya said Chester stopped by the Officer's Club virtually every evening for a coke, about ten minutes each time. Chester Garrett was an "extremely kind person". Montoya was having marital problems, and Chester talked her into trying to work things out with her husband. They met socially four or five times to discuss her marital issues. Bettie Montoya had no idea who might have killed Chester Garrett.

On July 26, Special Agent Gee verified through military Casualty Assistance Records that Chester Garrett had two civilian life insurance policies, amounts unknown, with Lisbeth, Roger and Patrick as beneficiaries.

Also on July 26, SA Gee interviewed CPT Woodrow McWilliams, who worked with MAJ Garrett from March 1975 until the Major died. CPT McWilliams described MAJ Garrett as "a super soldier" and extremely conscious of military bearing and protocol. McWilliams had seen MAJ Garrett angry on several occasions but doubted he would ever strike anyone. CPT McWilliams was a pallbearer at MAJ Garrett's funeral and commented that while Patrick was emotionally upset and taking the death of his father very hard, Lisbeth and Roger were quite casual and did not seem to be upset.

Also on July 26, FBI Special Agent John Fowkes interviewed Mrs. Jeroline Pletcher, a close friend of Sharon Turner. Mrs. Pletcher was present when MAJ Garrett and Sharon Turner first met at the Knight's Club near Bassett Center on September 17, 1976. MAJ Garrett asked Sharon to dance, and after that night they dated on a regular basis. Mrs. Pletcher described Sharon Turner as a very religious, trusting and naïve divorcee. Sharon told Jeroline that Chester Garrett told her he was single and had never been married. Sharon also told Jeroline while Chester "conducted himself as a perfect gentleman", he tried to induce her to have sex, which she rebuffed due to her strong religious beliefs. Mrs. Pletcher felt they were "truly in love." MAJ Garrett told both Sharon Turner and Jeroline he planned to marry Sharon and take her and her children with him when he was transferred to Italy in March 1977. Sharon bought herself a wedding dress in anticipation of the occasion after Chester asked her ring size.

On the same day, FBI Special Agent Wallace Crossmon interviewed Jerry Polanco, manager of the Howard Johnson's Motel on Interstate I-10, and recovered registration cards that verified Eugene Thomas' alibi for the evening of January 3.

On July 28, FBI Special Agent Kenneth Cooper interviewed Curtis Austin at Fort Bliss about his friend Donald Smith. Austin said he spoke with Donald Smith a few weeks before, who told him "some dudes" he played basketball with at William Beaumont Army Hospital were involved with the murder of a Major at Fort Bliss. Austin said after Donald Smith left the army Austin ran into another friend, Fresnel Sorel, who recounted how Donald Smith told him of the threat from the basketball players.

On July 29, Army CID Special Agent Gee, FBI Special Agent Beck and El Paso Sheriff's Sergeant Timmons interviewed Harry Snelson, father of Roger's friend Robert Snelson. Mr. Snelson repeated his prior statements about his son and Roger's encounters on January 3. Harry Snelson added that he did not particularly like Roger and felt that Roger, two years older than Robert, had too much influence on his son. For example, about a year earlier Robert allowed Roger to spend the night without knowledge or permission from Mr. Snelson. That night MAJ Garrett came over looking for Roger, and Mr. Snelson told him Roger was not there, and was upset the next morning when he learned Roger had been there all night.

On the same day, FBI Special Agent Wallace Crossmon interviewed Bertha Torres, who confirmed Eugene Thomas' alibi for January 3 by stating she and her girlfriend Irma Leal spent the night with Thomas and his buddy "Smitty" at Howard Johnson's Motel, she and Smitty in one room and Eugene and Irma in the other.

Also on July 29, FBI Special Agent Kenneth Cooper interviewed Wayne Rensen, a friend of Fresnel Sorel, who overheard Donald Smith's story of the threat against Smith and the threat to cut off Sorel's arm. Renson told SA Cooper he believed none of it; that Donald Smith was a kleptomaniac, a liar and a thief, and he believed nothing Smith had to say.

On July 31, Army CID Special Agent Gee and FBI Special Agent Beck interviewed Sharon Turner in Sunland Park, New Mexico. Sharon repeated Jeroline Pletcher's account of how she and Chester Garrett met at the Knight's Club in El Paso and how they began dating regularly. Sharon said Chester spoke of marriage within a week of meeting her and told her he was not married. She said Chester spoke of taking her with him to Italy, going house hunting in El Paso, and buying a wedding gown. Sharon described Chester Garrett as extremely physically fit, enthusiastic and aggressive.

Sharon Turner said that on January 3, she received a phone call from Chester about noontime, and she told him she was too tired to go out that night. She was surprised she did not hear from him that afternoon, as he usually called her each afternoon. He did call her between 8:20pm and 8:30pm, apologized for calling late and explained when he got home after basketball practice he realized he had Lieutenant Sherwin's car keys and had to return them. Chester Garrett went on to say he had to cut one of the basketball players from the team; a good player but with a bad attitude. She went to sleep after concluding the conversation.

Sharon Turner said she "felt uneasy" when she woke on the morning of January 4. She didn't receive a phone call from Chester all day, which was "extremely unusual." She thought perhaps he was tied up with the basketball team again.

Sharon said on January 5, about 7:30am, she received a call from Jerrie Pletcher and learned Chester had been killed and that he had a wife and two children. Sharon said she did not attend the funeral because she was "a good Christian" and it would have been inappropriate.

Chapter 32

Roger, Chester, Lisbeth, Patrick, circa 1971

From May 1971 through January 1972, MAJ Garrett returned to Ft Bragg and assumed command of an Operational Special Forces Company and subsequent staff position. In that staff position he was responsible for developing, preparing, and updating the U.S. Army portion of supporting joint unconventional warfare, direct action, stability operations, contingency and augmentation plans that dealt with tactical deployment and employment of U.S. Army Special Forces from the U.S. Army John F. Kennedy Center for Military Assistance (USAJFKCENMA) in the Middle East area. During this assignment he was also selected as the USAJFKCENMA Command Briefer as an additional duty because of his superior command presence and knowledge of Special Forces operations.

Chapter 33

On August 1, FBI Special Agent Beck and Army CID Special Agent Gee interviewed Robert Snelson, Roger's friend and neighbor, who again recounted Roger's visits to his house on January 3. Robert said he learned of MAJ Garrett's death the next day when he called Roger around 4pm or 5pm and Roger told Robert someone killed his father. Robert said Roger had not spoken much about his father's murder since. Robert said he was "not unaware" of why Mr. and Mrs. Garrett had marital difficulties, and noted it bothered Roger quite a bit that his parents didn't live together. Robert said Lisbeth kept "a very tight rein" on Roger. For example, while he was in band and football he was not allowed to take any school trips outside of El Paso. Robert said he felt Roger and MAJ Garrett didn't get along very well, and Roger "more or less tolerated" his father.

On August 3, Army CID Special Agent J.W. Gee interviewed CPT Isaac Diggs, who met MAJ Garrett in April 1976, and had daily professional contact with him until his death. CPT Diggs described MAJ Garrett as very conscientious and an excellent soldier. CPT Diggs indicated the only person he knew would have a reason to kill MAJ Garrett was Roosevelt Hill. MAJ Garrett and CPT Diggs were instrumental in "getting Hill busted out of the Army". CPT Diggs had witnessed several conversations between MAJ Garrett and Private Hill and noted that MAJ Garrett was verbally abusive to Hill and Hill greatly resented it.

Also on August 3, FBI Special Agent James Beck interviewed Irma Leal at FBI El Paso. Irma Leal, like Bertha Torres before her, corroborated Eugene Thomas' alibi for the night of January 3, saying she and Bertha met Eugene Thomas and his friend David Smith. They bought a bottle of liquor, checked into the Howard Johnson's Motel where they spent the night, Irma Leal with Eugene Thomas and Bertha Torres with David Smith.

On August 8, Army CID Special Agent Tim Weber interviewed 1st Lieutenant Karen McClellan at Fort Meade,

Maryland. 1LT McClellan also gave a written statement about her relationship with MAJ Chester Garrett. She said she met MAJ Garrett in July 1973 in Nakhon Phanom, Thailand, when he was assigned to the Joint Casualty Resolution Center with her brother, CPT John McClellan. Karen lived with her family in Bangkok: her father Major General Stan McClellan, her mother and brother. MAJ Garrett was a regular guest at their home. Karen McClellan said MAJ Garrett told her he was divorced, and they dated frequently as friends. McClellan stressed their relationship was never, in any way, intimate. MAJ Garret did ask her to marry him, but she was not interested in marriage. After MAJ Garrett left Thailand for Fort Bliss in October 1973 they corresponded regularly until she received a telephone call from Mrs. Garrett, who advised Karen she was divorcing Chester, after which they could marry. Karen was shocked to learn Chester was married, and made it clear she had no intention of marrying Chester Garrett whether he was married or not.

1LT Karen McClellan and MAJ Garrett reestablished contact months later. Chester told her he lied about being divorced as he knew she wouldn't date him otherwise, but he said he was legally separated after coming home from his second tour in Vietnam to find Lisbeth living with another man. Chester said he felt a great sense of personal failure over his marriage. He no longer cared for his wife but he loved his sons and didn't want to be separated from them. Still, his family treated him coldly. They didn't correspond with him in Thailand, nor had anyone met him upon his return to the United States. He moved into BOQ at Fort Bliss and asked for a divorce, but Lisbeth refused because she wanted his financial support. Chester told his wife he had fallen in love with a girl in Thailand. In December 1973 his BOQ room was broken into and money, a television set and some of Karen's letters were stolen. Because of the letters, Chester suspected Lisbeth was behind the theft.

1LT McClellan said her relationship with MAJ Garrett was shared by her entire family, who liked the Major very much. Chester was frustrated with the slowness of obtaining a divorce, and with trying to show his sons he loved them. Several months before his death, his room was broken into again, admittedly by Lisbeth. She took all of his plaques and awards on display, which hurt Chester greatly as he was very proud of his military career and loved the mementos. Lisbeth refused to return them.

1LT Karen McClellan last spoke to MAJ Garrett a few days before Christmas 1976. She said Chester was in excellent spirits, hopeful for a divorce and looking forward to his foreign assignment. He told Karen he hoped to remarry someday, hopefully someone with children from a previous marriage because he liked children very much.

Karen McClellan described Chester Garrett as one of the kindest people she had ever met and considered by his peers and subordinates to be the perfect soldier and man.

Also on August 8, FBI Special Agent James Beck called Army CID Special Agent J.W. Gee and advised he had been contacted by El Paso Drug Enforcement Administration (DEA) with information from December 1976. DEA told SA Beck that retired Army Colonel Joseph Hornisher contacted DEA and said MAJ Garrett was involved in drug trafficking, and DEA had passed the information to the El Paso County Sheriff's Department in January 1977.

Chapter 34

In July 1972, Chester Garrett began his 3rd Combat tour in Vietnam as a Senior Advisor with HQ's Army Advisory Group, Military Assistance Command, Vietnam (MACV). Garrett joined the unit while it was on a combat operation near Quang Tri, Vietnam. He was quick to establish a strong rapport with his Battalion Commander and was able to make timely recommendations on maneuver and fire support. Garrett's sound advice and professional competence greatly assisted his unit as it attacked into a heavily defended enemy base area. The unit seized its objectives and inflicted heavy casualties on a large enemy force while sustaining only minor losses themselves.

By this point the Vietnamese war had become incredibly unpopular in the United States. In January 1973, after months of negotiations, representatives of the United States, North Vietnam, South Vietnam and the Vietcong signed a peace agreement in Paris. A primary condition of the agreement was the withdrawal of American forces from Vietnam.

Chester Garrett was caught by troop withdrawal, but instead of shipping home, he was sent to Thailand in February 1973, to join the newly formed Joint Casualty Resolution Center (JCRC), created as the United States prepared its exit from Vietnam. Article 8(b) of the Paris Accords dealt with the resolution of the fate of those Americans and others unaccounted for at the conclusion of hostilities. Article 8(b), states:

> "The parties shall help each other to get information about those military personnel and civilians of the parties missing in action, to determine the location and take care of the graves of the dead so as to facilitate the exhumation and repatriation of the remains, and to take any such other measures as may be required to get information about those still considered missing in action.
>
> "JCRC was established as an operational element

on January 23, 1973, with Brigadier General Robert C. Kingston as commander. JCRC's mission was to assist Secretaries of the Armed Services in resolving the fate of servicemen missing and unaccounted for as a result of hostilities throughout Indochina. JCRC was to conduct field searches, excavations, recovery, and repatriation activities negotiated through the Four Party Joint Military Team (FPJMT). FPJMT's specific responsibility was to search and account for missing individuals, and had representation from the United States, South Vietnam, North Vietnam and the Viet Cong. The U.S. delegation to the FPJMT became, in essence, a negotiating entity to barter with North Vietnamese and Viet Cong officials in locating MIAs. U.S. personnel initially assigned to the JCRC were from Special Forces. General Kingston personally interviewed each volunteer, accepting those whose talents matched skill sets needed to perform the mission. The personnel roster, with an initial authorization of approximately 140 persons, was heavily loaded on the side of field search teams. JCRC was activated in Vietnam but was soon moved to Nakhon Phanom Air Base in Thailand due to U.S. interpretation of Paris Accord restrictions on the number of U.S. military personnel in Vietnam.

"Major Garrett served as a Control Team Operations Officer. He was responsible for planning, implementing and supervising the training program for the Forward Operating Base and its assigned Field Teams. He commanded, organized and trained field operational elements for Casualty Resolution Operations in Cambodia and Laos."

Apparently, Garrett impressed his superiors at the Casualty Resolution Operations, for the Lieutenant Colonel rater for his OER wrote:

"Major Garrett is the finest Major in the U.S. Army. No one is more conscientious or hard working. He has no peer as an organizer, can get to the meat of any problem in minutes. He is completely honest and frank. He loves the Army and is probably in the finest physical condition of any officer in the U.S.A. He is extremely intelligent, writes and speaks well. Major Garrett was charged with the responsibility of writing a Standard Operating Procedure and establishing a training program to prepare field teams for operations in Cambodia and Laos. He accomplished this and more. This officer has General Officer potential. He should be promoted immediately, sent to the Command and General Staff College as soon as possible, selected for civilian schooling, and assigned to positions of great responsibility."

Chapter 35

On September 20, FBI Special Agent Gary Webb called Army CID Special Agent Gee and advised that Donald Smith twice failed to appear for scheduled interviews with FBI New York. SA Webb further advised he was coordinating with the El Paso United States Attorney's Office to obtain a federal arrest warrant for Donald Smith for the theft of the government typewriter. SA Webb asked SA Gee to contact his CID counterparts in Germany and request they interview PFC Roderick Gathright.

Donald Smith was arrested on a federal warrant for theft of government property in New York and transported to El Paso, where on October 7 he appeared before Federal Magistrate Judge Harry Hudspeth for his preliminary and detention hearings and released on a $25,000 bond.

Chapter 36

Army Commendation Medal – 2nd Oak Leaf Cluster with V/Device
Vietnamese Gallantry Cross with Silver Star

On November 25, 1972, during Operation LAMSON 72, Major Garrett was serving as Senior Advisor to the 5th Airborne Battalion of the Army of the Republic of Vietnam on a ground reconnaissance operation in the Quang Tri Province. As evening approached, Major Garrett's unit ceased patrol and were establishing a night defensive position when a booby trap exploded, killing two Vietnamese soldiers and wounding nine more. The unit froze, fearing additional booby traps. Major Garrett immediately moved into the scene, and with a flashlight personally cleared the position after finding and disarming two additional booby traps. Then he turned his attention to wounded; applying first aid and assisting in their evacuation, undoubtedly contributing to the survival of several of the wounded.

For his actions, Major Garrett was awarded his second Army Commendation Medal with V/Device and the Republic of Vietnam Gallantry Cross with Silver Star.

Chapter 37

On October 20, a significant teletype was sent from the Director of the FBI to the Special Agent in Charge of FBI El Paso. The teletype read as follows:

"The Behavioral Science Unit, Training Division, has reviewed material sent with referenced airtel and has arrived at the following conclusions:

"The attack upon the victim, while brutal, does not necessarily indicate rage. The stab wounds are not excessive in number, and the blow to the skull, while obviously quite forceful, does not necessarily indicate the often excessive violence found in an assault predicated upon rage. The disposal of the body in the backseat of the victim's auto, abandoned relatively near his home with the door locked and the keys missing, is noteworthy. It would indicate that at least two persons shared in the disposal of the victim. Further, the locked door and missing keys would indicate the perpetrators, or at least those who disposed of the body, had a rather "proprietary" interest in the auto. It is not uncommon for an individual under a great deal of pressure to return to "habits" engrained earlier in their development.

"Considering the victim's violent temper as was set forth in his psychiatric examinations as well as his excellent physical condition, it is not difficult to fit the facts as presented to the Behavioral Science Unit into the following scenario: An individual, naïve or inexperienced insofar as violence is concerned, perhaps spurred on by some threat such as the victim's show of violent temper, strikes the victim in the head and knocks him down. Then realizing that the victim is not immediately rendered unconscious and is defending himself from further blows, the attacker panics and stabs the victim until the victim is not moving.

"Considering the relationship victim had with his wife and stepson, as well as the above scenario, it would not do to eliminate those two as suspects. The Behavioral Science Unit would recommend that the young stepson be approached separately from his mother, if possible, in the event you are able to question him further."

Chapter 38

Private First Class Roderick Gathright was interviewed by Army CID in Schweinfurt, Germany on November 1 and November 9. During his first interview PFC Gathright appeared calm and cooperative but non-committal and denied any knowledge of Garrett's death or what part his cousin Eugene Thomas may have played in his death. During the second interview Gathright vacillated between apathy and outright hostility, enough to cause the interviewer concern. On November 15, Special Agent Gee received a telephone call from CID Schweinfurt stating they believed Gathright was dishonest and deceptive, and was probably involved in the murder along with Eugene Thomas and Donald Smith.

On November 3, Donald Smith and Roderick Gathright were indicted for the stolen typewriter by a federal Grand Jury in El Paso. On November 15, FBI Special Agent Gary Webb and Army CID Special Agent J.W. Gee briefed Assistant U.S. Attorney Stanley Serwatka on Gathright's interviews in Germany. AUSA Serwatka advised he planned to offer Donald Smith immunity from the typewriter case in exchange for relevant information on Garrett's murder. Serwatka also stated his intent to extradite Gathright to El Paso and offer him the same deal if Donald Smith refused to cooperate.

On November 21, Army CID Special Agent J.W. Gee was contacted by MAJ Ralph Mitchell of the Fort Bliss Provost Marshal's Office about two letters MAJ Mitchell received from a Sergeant Harlan Irons stationed in Germany. SGT Irons wrote that he knew MAJ Garrett from the gym at Fort Bliss, and that Garrett told him once in 1976 two people were out to kill the Major because he had "busted them" for drugs and for going AWOL. The letters were postmarked November 8 and November 9.

On November 23, FBI Special Agent Gary Webb and Army CID Special Agent J.W Gee interviewed Doctor Joseph Hornisher, who said the female manager of the Fort Bliss Officers' Club told him about a week after MAJ Garrett's death that he was killed because he was to be a witness against persons involved in drug trafficking at Fort Bliss. The Special Agents tracked down the Officers' Club manager, who turned out to be Bettie Montoya, as SA Gee suspected, since he had interviewed her in July. Two days later, he and SA Webb interviewed Montoya again, who provided essentially the same information as she had in July. Bettie Montoya did not recall making any comments about MAJ Garrett's involvement with drug traffickers and denied any knowledge of Garrett using or being involved with drugs.

Chapter 39

On December 15, Donald Smith was interviewed by FBI Special Agent Gary Webb and Assistant U.S. Attorney Rusty Guyer as witnessed by Smith's Public Defender attorney Herbert Cooper. AUSA Guyer offered Donald Smith immunity in the typewriter case if he would provide information on MAJ Garrett's murder. Donald Smith denied any knowledge of MAJ Garrett's murder and admitted he made up the story about "Gene and Jeff" threatening to cut off Fresnel Sorel's arm to gain Sorel's sympathy about Smith's debt owed to Sorel.

Chapter 40

Vietnamese Gallantry Cross with Gold Star

During November 1972, Major Garrett was Senior Advisor to the 5th Airborne Battalion of the Army of the Republic of Vietnam, and led Operation LAMSON 72/Dai Bang 72 operations in the Quang Tri and Thue Thien Provinces. On November 19 and 22, Major Garrett's unit made fierce contact with Viet Cong units. Despite intense hostile fire on both occasions, Major Garrett calmly coordinated accurate allied artillery fire and the operational objective was captured. Major Garrett's actions resulted in 42 enemy soldiers killed and the capture of one 130mm gun, two heavy automatic rifles, six B40 weapons, twenty AK-47 rifles and an important amount of documents and support equipment.

For his actions Major Garrett was awarded the Republic of Vietnam Gallantry Cross with Gold Star.

Chapter 41

On January 18, 1978, PFC Roderick Gathright arrived in El Paso after being extradited from Germany. The next day he appeared before a federal magistrate judge, who released Gathright to Fort Bliss Military Police on a $10,000 bond.

On January 23, 1978, one year and twenty days after MAJ Garrett was killed, CID Special Agent J.W. Gee wrote a five page summary report of the major events and evidence recovered concerning the investigation. In the last two paragraphs SA Gee wrote:

"They (FBI) plan to refer the entire matter to the U.S. Attorney's Office, El Paso, TX, recommending a special grand jury to be convened to hear all aspects of this investigation. The FBI presently feels that the most productive side of this investigation is the suspected involvement of Ann and Roger GARRETT in the death of MAJ GARRETT. However, the FBI presently lacks the investigative jurisdiction to pursue leads pertaining to Ann and Roger GARRETT. This jurisdiction could be provided by the Justice Department should any indictments be returned on Ann and Roger Garrett by the proposed Grand Jury.

"On 24 Jan 78, at 0900, SA Gary K. Webb, Special Agent, FBI, El Paso, TX, advised that his office would formally assume all investigative jurisdiction in this investigation. SA Webb was provided appropriate information regarding all outstanding investigative interviews."

////////////////////LAST ENTRY////////////////////

Chapter 42

Meritorious Service Medal (posthumous)

The Meritorious Service Medal was the last military decoration to be awarded to Major Garrett, posthumously in 1977. The citation reads:

"TO Major Chester Garrett, Infantry, FOR exceptionally meritorious service in successive positions of great responsibility. While serving with the Special Forces Group as Regional Forces/Popular Forces Advisor in the Republic of Vietnam, MAJ Garrett was responsible for completely reorganizing and revitalizing the district intelligence net and instilling courage and aggressiveness in the RVN forces. By personal example of tenacity and heroism, he inspired his counterparts to become one of the finest fighting forces in the country. MAJ Garrett continued to serve with distinction in the Southeast and subsequently in the U.S. Army Air Defense School, where his wide troop and combat experience enabled him to contribute immeasurably to the development of troop-oriented programs and a direct increase in battalion morale. His exemplary service reflects distinct credit upon himself and the United Sates Army."

The Meritorious Service Medal is awarded to members of the Armed Forces of the United States who distinguished themselves by outstanding non-combat meritorious achievement or service to the United States subsequent to 16 January 1969. Normally, the acts or services rendered must be comparable to that required for the Legion of Merit but in a duty of lesser though considerable responsibility.

Chapter 43

Barely 100 days after Army CID SA Gee's summary report of January 23, 1978, on May 9, 1978, FBI closed its investigation based on its inability to prove basketball players murdered Chester Garrett. The EPSD and Army CID cases lay stagnant as each new day brought fresh cases of murder, rape, kidnapping and other violent crimes. Whatever good intentions investigators held for Chester Garrett, those involved were promoted, transferred, retired or died. The frantic inertia from 1977 slowly lost momentum and finally stopped altogether.

At this stage there were two schools of thought between the three agencies: either Lisbeth and Roger killed Chester Garrett or the black soldiers in question from Fort Bliss did it. FBI and Army CID pursued the soldiers while the Sheriff's Department concentrated on Lisbeth and Roger.

Sheriff's Department detectives who saw Muriatic Acid stains in the driveway of 1349 Backus on January 13 knew Lisbeth and Roger did it. Furthermore, they knew Eugene Thomas and Howard Jackson both had solid alibis for the night of the murder. So when the detectives were kicked out of 1349 Backus by Lisbeth's attorney after seeing acid stains and flecks of blood in the garage and kitchen, why didn't they immediately secure a search warrant for the residence?

It's difficult to determine from a vantage point of forty years later, but the failure of the District Attorney's Office to quickly indict and prosecute Lisbeth and Roger was likely due to a variety of issues.

Consider for a moment the jurisdictional and cultural differences between the agencies involved in this investigation:

The Federal Bureau of Investigation has been a top level agency since it was formed in 1908 to combat organized crime. When the FBI speaks, other agencies tend to pause and take note. They have the largest and highest-tech criminal laboratory in the world, a world-wide reputation for excellence, and a huge budget to ensure quality results.

The mission of the United States Attorney's Office's (USAO) is to prosecute federal crimes brought to their office by federal law enforcement agencies. The USAO was minimally involved in the Garrett investigation because the El Paso Sheriff's Department was the lead agency, and their cases are usually prosecuted by the El Paso County District Attorney's Office. The USAO and FBI traditionally work very closely on any FBI investigation. The USAO did work the stolen government property angle of the case, mostly in an attempt to force cooperation from soldiers and former soldiers in the FBI investigation.

The Army's CID is also a federal agency. Composed of military and civilian investigators, Army CID has limited jurisdiction and a limited budget. Army CID rarely works with the United States Attorney's Office as most of their "clients" are prosecuted under the Uniform Code of Military Justice rather than civilian United States Code, but it can happen.

El Paso County Sheriff's Department's jurisdiction is limited to El Paso County. Sheriff's deputies traditionally start out as detention officers working in the county jail for a few months or years before becoming a uniform deputy patrolling the county. Detectives are promoted from the uniform ranks for different units, in this case the Crimes Against Persons unit which investigates complex crimes including murder. Generally, uniform officers who make detective in any agency are a cut above the average uniform cop, but as in any specific group of humans anywhere, there are good, average and poor performers. Homicide detectives are often the sharpest minds in any given law enforcement agency, not only because of the seriousness of that offense, but also due to the high profile public arena in which they often work.

The mission of the El Paso District Attorney's Office is to prosecute cases under state and county statutes brought to them by the El Paso Sheriff's Department and El Paso Police Department. While technically the DA's office and the Sheriff's Department are separate county entities, symbiotic cooperation between ADAs and EPSD CAP detectives are vital to prosecute criminals in complex investigations.

Recent interviews with several original investigators have revealed an unusually good working relationship between these agencies. EPSD CAP was the lead agency and was not intimidated by "the feds". Investigators from EPSD CAP, Army CID and FBI routinely partnered for interviews and constantly shared information and planned strategy.

Mistakes were made, however, and there were some internal issues and restrictions.

Army CID Special Agent J.W. Gee believed Lisbeth and Roger killed Chester Garrett, but he was mandated to follow orders from his chain of command. SA Gee was frustrated by CID's jurisdiction limitations. An example is the report he filed on January 19, 1977, after being ordered to shut down the Garrett investigation. Army CID's policy was to cease investigative activity when a lead went off military property or away from an active duty soldier. Although SA Gee officially closed the case as ordered, he was almost immediately drawn back into it with his superior's blessings. Certainly, every single lead in a murder investigation needs to be followed, but it is possible that Army CID command pursued the black soldier suspects long after they should have been ruled out because it was the only legal avenue available for them to work.

The El Paso FBI's insistence on proving the black soldiers' involvement in Chester Garrett's murder is puzzling. It may have seemed attractive in the beginning as it promised to lead into drug trafficking and theft of government property. Even after FBI's Behavioral Science Unit sent a teletype to FBI El Paso in September speculating the murderers were Lisbeth and Roger, and after another teletype from the FBI Director to the Special Agent in Charge (SAC) of FBI El Paso noting "wife and stepson should not be eliminated" as suspects, FBI El Paso still followed the trail of a stolen typewriter in hopes of solving the murder. This is evidenced in an interesting letter in May 1978, from El Paso FBI to El Paso United States Attorney's Office stating that FBI initially identified Donald Smith, Roderick Gathright, Eugene Thomas and Howard Jackson as suspects in the Garrett murder but were "unable to obtain any direct evidence." The letter also stated Smith and Gathright were indicted for Theft of Government Property, had gone to trial in El Paso and were both acquitted. The Acting SAC advised "no further investigation will be conducted by the FBI and this matter will be placed in a closed status." The FBI did not solely concentrate on the soldiers, as evidenced by FBI SA Gary Webb's and FBI SA James

Beck's exhaustive efforts and coordination with EPSD to investigate Lisbeth and Roger Garrett, but the soldiers quickly became the Bureau's primary focus.

EPSD essentially solved the case within two weeks, but apparently the facts of the case were not made known to, or were perhaps ignored by, the DA's Office, U.S. Attorney's Office, Army CID and FBI. Assistant DA John Cowan was present at the consent search of 1349 Backus on January 13, was aware of acid stains and blood spatter, was kicked out of the house with the detectives, and apparently advised Sergeant Fred Timmons he would secure a search warrant, but it didn't happen.

Detective John Omohundro wrote the following report after the consent search at 1349 Backus:

> "Jan. 13, 1977 (THURSDAY)
> "11:30 am Undersigned officer obtained a statement from Lisbeth Garrett in the presence of her attorney Mike Cohen. Undersigned obtained a consent to search her house and vehicle. (attached to case).
> "2:10 pm Undersigned officer and Ranger Pete Montemayor arrived at 1349 Backus and awaited the arrival of other investigating officers. Sergeant Timmons was already present at the address and Officers Brown, Reyes, Gomez, and ID&R officer Gurrola arrived and officers began to search the residence with the assistance of ADA John Cowan. Officer Jesus Reyes obtained several items of evidence as officers noticed what appeared to be blood on the south wall of the garage. The attorneys for Garrett and Mrs. Garrett were present.
> "5:00 pm Officers completed their search and departed the scene.
> …Investigation continues…..
> John Omohundro, Criminal Division"

Detective Omohundro's very short report did not document that he saw dried blood on the wall in the dining area under the table nor that consent was denied immediately after seeing the dried blood spatter.

Forty-one years later, former Assistant DA John Cowan remembered visiting the house with the detectives after being requested by EPSD to attend in hope of establishing good probable cause for any potential arrest warrants or search warrants. Upon arrival, ADA Cowan realized Attorney Michael Cohen was present for the Garrett family, and ADA Cowan felt they were not receiving full cooperation from MAJ Garrett's wife and children. In particular, ADA Cowan sensed Lisbeth was a "cold, calculating and rough" individual. ADA Cowan also noted the garage was sterile and tidy, and remembered some possible blood spatter in the garage, but he did not remember any blood in the kitchen under the dining room table. Nor did former ADA John Cowan remember meeting with the detectives in front of the house after they were kicked out, or any intent to pursue a search warrant afterwards. John Cowan's opinion for all of these years has been that they secured all possible evidence during the consent search, and it was simply not enough for the DA's Office to prosecute anyone, even though everyone involved from the EPSD and DA's Office believed Lisbeth and Roger were the guilty parties.

Interviews with surviving investigators of this case revealed some antagonism within EPSD CID itself at that time. Sheriff Mike Sullivan personally hired Mac Stout, a former Texas Ranger, to be captain in charge of CID. That appointment rankled Sergeant Fred Timmons, who probably felt he should have been CID captain. Multiple sources have indicated Sheriff Sullivan and Captain Stout were good friends and drinking buddies. Sergeant Timmons believed in rank-and-file leadership, and became incensed when Captain Stout routinely overruled Sergeant Timmons' management decisions. In fact, Captain Stout was known to delegate Sergeant Timmons to basic investigative roles in some cases, including this one. Multiple detectives said Sergeant Timmons had a heavy-handed "my way or the highway" approach to management, which restricted free flow of communication between ranks. On the other hand, the CAP detectives said they were extremely close with each other, "like brothers", because of the constantly shared experience of attempting great feats with far too few personnel and chafing together under experiences of perceived mismanagement. The detectives cared for each other, looked out for each other, and cared for each other's families in time of need, which was often.

However, all of the EPSD detectives interviewed agree on one thing: when they were kicked out of the house, they gathered in front down by the street. Sergeant Fred Timmons advised that ADA John Cowan was departing for his office to secure a search warrant. Sergeant Timmons further ordered the detectives to return to the CAP office and await the search warrant, which they did. The search warrant never materialized. The detectives offered opinions, including a possible close personal relationship between Lisbeth's attorney Michael Cohen and the DA's Office, but it's doubtful we will ever determine why a search warrant was not issued.

So why did this investigation go nowhere in 1977? Was it bad feelings, or too heavy a work load, within EPSD CAP itself? Was it poor communication between law enforcement agencies? Why did FBI El Paso ignore hints from its own Behavioral Science Unit and from the FBI Director himself? Why did the DA's Office insist on presenting Lisbeth and Roger before the Grand Jury prematurely and without physical evidence? Why didn't they secure a search warrant after being kicked out of the Garrett residence?

Frankly, these questions are completely unfair to ask decades after Chester Garrett's murder on January 3, 1977. Any person who has led a complex investigation knows how unreasonable it is to have decisions, made under stress and without complete knowledge of a situation, questioned later under a microscope in full light of day. The authors, having exhaustively researched the incredible life and bizarre death of MAJ Chester Garrett, know to lay blame for an unfinished investigation on any certain agency or group of investigators is utter nonsense. It is clear the investigators and prosecutors were competent. Some were more intuitive than others, some were better writers, and some were simply sharper. But no evidence would indicate sabotage, incompetence, or corruption.

Still, the unfair question nags at everyone involved. What exactly ran this case off the road and into the ditch? We'll probably never know and each year there are fewer living witnesses who could tell us.

Part 2
Creed of the Homicide Investigators of Texas

No Greater Honor will ever be bestowed on you as a Police Officer or a more Profound Duty imposed on you than when you are entrusted with the investigation of the death of a human being. It is the moral duty and, as an Officer entrusted with such a duty, it is incumbent upon you to follow the course of events and the facts as they develop to their ultimate conclusion. It is a heavy responsibility. As such, let no person deter you from the truth or your personal conviction to see that justice is done, not only for the deceased, but for the surviving family as well.

Chapter 44

Sgt. James Belknap, supervisor of the EPSO Crimes Against Persons-Major Crimes Section for 16 years

In April of 2006, Sergeant James Belknap was in charge of El Paso Sheriff's Office (EPSO, changed from the prior "El Paso Sheriff's Department") Crimes Against Persons. The unit was busier than ever. A spike in missing persons and homicides on both sides of the border had begun as skirmishes occurred across the river in Ciudad Juarez between two competing drug cartels. CAP was a busy unit.

One day Sergeant Belknap received a telephone call from a woman requesting an update on the unsolved murder of her brother, Chester Garrett. She identified herself as Jackie Conner and advised Sergeant Belknap her brother, Chester Garrett, was killed in 1977 and to date the case remained unsolved. Jackie also indicated she had additional information to share with investigators. Sergeant Belknap told Jackie he would have a detective contact her as soon as possible.

That detective was Antonio Arias. "Tony" Arias was a senior detective who joined EPSO in 1984, did about a year as a county jail detention officer and then uniform deputy patrol duty in the county before becoming a detective in 1989. Tony Arias was born to be a detective. Quiet by nature but a sharp observer of human nature,

Detective Arias was soon solving complex cases of murder, kidnapping and assault in a manner that made him a natural leader in the pool of CAP investigators and one of Sergeant Belknap's "go-to" guys.

However, Detective Arias was more than a little overwhelmed when Sergeant Belknap assigned this 29-year-old cold murder case to him. He knew time was a foreboding enemy. The first few days are the prime time to solve a major crime against a victim. The window of opportunity begins to close rapidly on any investigation, as investigators found in 1977. Tony rolled up his sleeves and pored over the Garrett investigation in addition to his already heavy case load. Most immediate, and unknown, were the current states of original witnesses and evidence. It seemed a daunting endeavor. No indictments, no arrests, and seemingly no leads. The case went cold…ice cold.

In 1977-1978, most leads pointed to Lisbeth and Roger Garrett as primary suspects in Chester Garrett's murder. After studying the electronic case file, Detective Tony Arias agreed. His first step was to check Roger and Lisbeth's criminal history since 1977. Lisbeth was clean, but Roger had an interesting series of collisions with the law. In July 1979, he was convicted on a charge of "Burglary Building", and sentenced to ten years' probation. In August 1983, he was convicted of "Delivery of Controlled Substance (Cocaine)" and given 150 days in prison. Two months later, he was sent to "Shock Probation" at Texas Department of Corrections (TDC). Shock Probation is a type of "scared straight" program that sometimes helps reform prisoners and prevents recidivism. In July 1985, Roger returned to state prison for unnamed probation violations. In October 1986, he was released to a halfway house in El Paso County, Texas. Roger was released from parole in May 1996, in spite of a June 1991 conviction on a charge of "Possession of Marijuana (less than 2 ounces)."

On May 1, 2006, Detective Arias called Jackie Conner, Chester Garrett's sister, and explained he was assigned to work her brother's murder investigation. Detective Arias could sense her frustration as she made it abundantly clear neither she nor her family had forgotten, or would ever forget, her brother's killers had not been brought to justice. Detective Arias could not help but admire Jackie's devotion and persistence by reaching out for answers almost 30 years after her brother's death.

Detective Arias explained to Jackie Conner that until recently he had been unaware of MAJ Garrett's murder, but he had reviewed the case file and was familiarizing himself with every detail. Jackie said Chester's youngest son, Patrick, had recently communicated with her and her sisters after several years of no contact. According to Jackie, Patrick told her two sisters, Cheryl and Gretchen, that his older brother Roger Garrett and his mother, Lisbeth Garrett, both confessed to Patrick their participation in Chester's murder. Patrick added Lisbeth had cancer and was on her deathbed when she made her confession.

Jackie Conner told Tony that Patrick said Roger told him he struck Chester with a baseball bat and stabbed him with a knife. Roger disposed of the bat and knife, as well as the tires on Lisbeth's vehicle as Roger knew the police would try to compare them with tire tracks found at the crime scene.

Jackie said she and her sisters had always suspected Lisbeth and Roger Garrett as being responsible for Chester's death. They also believed Patrick was not involved, mostly because Patrick was only twelve at the time. When pressed by his aunts if he had contacted law enforcement concerning these confessions, Patrick gave conflicting stories. One was he was waiting for his mother to die before filing charges against Roger. Patrick would inherit his mother's money and share it with his aunts. Another version Patrick gave was he had contacted law enforcement and an investigation was already underway.

Jackie Conner said approximately one year after Patrick had reunited with the sisters, he fell out of favor with them over a house in Las Vegas, Nevada, that Patrick rented from his aunt Gretchen. Jackie indicated that Gretchen and Patrick were no longer speaking. At this point, Patrick would not speak of Lisbeth and Roger's confessions any more. Jackie said Patrick never showed any proof of having contacted police.

Jackie Conner recalled how Lisbeth was elegantly dressed in a black veil and hat at Chester's funeral. Jackie could not comprehend how one day Chester was found murdered, and the next Lisbeth could go shopping for an entire outfit to wear at the funeral. Jackie insisted she did not see Lisbeth shed a tear during the funeral. After the funeral, the family went to Lisbeth's home and Jackie's older brother, Dino, became upset when he saw Roger laughing and carrying on as if nothing had happened. Jackie also recalled Roger commenting on how hard Chester's head was as he told a story about Chester falling from a cliff in Panama, hitting his head and not sustaining any type of injury. At the time the comment meant nothing to Jackie; only later, when she read the autopsy report that listed Chester's cause of death as a fractured skull, did the comment seem significant.

    Jackie Conner said Lisbeth never once said she missed Chester or made any effort to find his killer. In Jackie's eyes, Lisbeth acted as if she were never married to Chester. A few months later, Lisbeth informed Jackie she had purchased a new home, which sparked a thought that Lisbeth might be responsible for her brother's murder. Jackie said she last spoke to Lisbeth about May 1977. When Detective Arias told Jackie he intended to interview her sisters, Jackie also provided contact information to reach her daughter, Maureen Vidmar, who had also been in contact with Patrick via e-mail. Jackie added Patrick had also told Maureen of his mother's and brother's confessions to him.

Chapter 45

On that same day Detective Tony Arias contacted and spoke with Chester and Jackie's sister, Gretchen Smith. Gretchen said that in July or August of 2004, she received a phone call from her nephew, Patrick Garrett. She had not seen or spoken to Patrick since Chester's funeral in 1977, some 27 years before. Patrick told her he had been trying to contact his father's side of the family, but his mother Lisbeth would not allow it. Patrick informed Gretchen he was living in Missouri but planned to move to Las Vegas, where she lived, as he had recently lost his job. They communicated several times by telephone, and it was during one of those calls when Patrick first told Gretchen that Roger confessed he killed their father. Patrick also described his mother as "consumed with guilt" over the murder, and had become a recluse. Patrick explained his mother was ill with cancer and he planned to wait until her death to turn Roger in to authorities. Gretchen told Detective Arias she and Patrick were no longer speaking. Issues over the rental house and other family matters caused a rift between them. Gretchen said she believed Patrick was a liar and a con man.

Gretchen recalled Lisbeth as icy and showing no emotion at Chester's funeral. After the funeral, Lisbeth told Gretchen that Chester had returned from Vietnam a changed man who was physically abusive towards her and her sons. Around this time, Gretchen's mother Adina sent a letter to Lisbeth informing her she was going to hire a detective to investigate Chester's death. Lisbeth immediately confronted Gretchen and her mother and made it very clear they had better leave things alone or whoever killed Chester would come after them. Gretchen took Lisbeth's statement as a threat.

Chapter 46

A critical component of any investigation is the integrity of chain-of-custody of evidence. CAP cleaned an empty office to make a sterile evidence vault solely dedicated to the Garrett investigation. All physical evidence available was gathered by the detectives, examined, re-examined, re-inventoried, stored and secured in that room. Now the detectives had instant and easy access to the collection and could learn it intimately, which sparked creative brain-storming and allowed them to prioritize re-testing certain items with more modern technology. The door lock was changed and the sole key was secured. A sign-in sheet was installed so anyone entering had to sign, date and time their purpose for entering. Evidence was stored in that manner for some six months before being returned to normal Evidence lockup.

Tony Arias arranged for DNA Analyst Christine Ceniceros from the Texas Department of Public Safety (DPS) Laboratory to review and evaluate evidence for its potential of extracting DNA. Tony had worked with Ms. Ceniceros previously and had complete confidence in her ability and professional opinions. Ms. Ceniceros selected specific items she thought had the highest probability of yielding DNA. The items were submitted to the DPS lab for analysis, and any resulting DNA signatures would be subjected to profiling processes to identify possible suspects.

One limitation of DNA analysis resulted from the original FBI examination of evidence in 1977. The process used then obliterated much of the submitted samples, so in 2006, it was necessary to pull "new" samples from whatever evidence remained.

The lengthy passage of time created issues. A major headache was that the original paper case file was missing. In the 1970s, case files were a collection of paper reports, paper witness statements, paper interview notes and paper photographs, usually stored in folders or cardboard boxes. The Chester Garrett file was not in the file room with the other old paper files. There were copies of some old Garrett reports in the electronic file, but it was by no means complete. Tony's biggest fear was the original had been misplaced into some old filing cabinet long since discarded.

Another evidence issue to contend with was MAJ Garrett's red Volkswagen Beetle. It was no longer in evidence. It was no longer anywhere in EPSO custody. It was simply…gone. The only part of the Volkswagen in evidence was the steering wheel, which had been removed for fingerprint analysis in 1977. The electronic case file indicated the vehicle had been stored at "El Paso Wrecker Service". In 2006, El Paso Wrecker Service was still in business, but they had no record of the Volkswagen. Ownership of El Paso Wrecker Service had changed some years before. Possibly records were lost or destroyed during the transition. CAP Detective Irene Anchondo physically inspected each vehicle on the lot; the Volkswagen was not there. Detective Arias contacted every officer he could find connected with the case in 1977 with no results.

Every vehicle produced or registered in the United States is assigned an exclusive Vehicle Identification Number (VIN) which indicates the car's specifications and manufacturer, and is used to monitor its history of ownership and registration. Chester Garrett's Volkswagen VIN search revealed zero history after 1977. The EPSO was never able to determine what happened to the vehicle.

Chapter 47

On June 3, 2006, Detective Arias contacted Maureen Vidmar, Jackie Conner's daughter and Patrick Garrett's cousin. Maureen said she heard from a cousin, Tammy Marie Smith, who said their mutual cousin, Patrick Garrett, had information relating to the death of his father, Chester Garrett. After hearing this, Maureen contacted Patrick. They communicated mostly by e-mail and during an e-mail exchange Patrick informed Maureen that while his mother Lisbeth was hospitalized with liver cancer, Patrick told her he had a right to know what had happened to his father. Patrick explained to Maureen he had always suspected his mother and brother of killing his father. Maureen told Detective Arias that Patrick told her his mother confirmed his suspicions. Patrick explained to Maureen he was at the movies with a friend that night. Patrick did not provide Maureen any more details but made it clear her family should not get involved and should remain quiet about the matter as he was already in contact with police and the FBI. Maureen told Tony Arias she exchanged e-mails with Patrick about the murder over a span of one week.

Maureen said her communication with Patrick tapered off and stopped. Maureen shut down her e-mail account altogether; she no longer had access to email messages between herself and Patrick.

Detective Arias realized he had to act quickly to try to preserve the email messages. Online service providers differ in how they retain email records. Some keep records indefinitely, some for a set period, and others don't retain any records. Detective Arias sent a "Preservation Letter" to Maureen's and Patrick's online providers, requesting preservation of any electronic records and stored communications to or from Maureen's or Patrick's email addresses. He also requested Grand Jury Subpoenas for the same information through the District Attorney's Office.

A Preservation Letter is a professional request from law enforcement to a company or person to retain and provide certain records. It has no legal authority but is quick and easy to serve. Grand Jury Subpoenas are legally binding orders that are issued after the District Attorney makes a formal presentation to a Grand Jury and receives a True Bill. Grand Jury Subpoenas are more difficult to obtain, but legally compel the recipient to present requested records to the Grand Jury within a certain time frame.

Now Tony Arias had to locate and interview numerous witnesses after almost three decades. With assistance from other CAP detectives, he initially used commercial and open source databases that collect personal information from public records. Most of the information was fragmented and obsolete, so more digging was required. In some cases detectives located witnesses through relatives whose information was more current. They also used state and federal law enforcement intelligence centers with analysts and databases dedicated to locating individuals.

On June 12, 2006, Tony Arias contacted another of Chester Garrett's sisters, Cheryl Ellington. Cheryl said she last saw her brother at the Officer's Club at Fort Bliss, about two weeks before his death. Cheryl explained she was with a date and Chester was with his girlfriend Sharon, but she could not recall Sharon's last name. Cheryl recalled Chester telling her at that time he was happy because he was going to finally be divorced from his wife Lisbeth in a couple of weeks, and he planned to marry Sharon. Cheryl Ellington said when her family was informed of Chester' death, they were completely devastated. She remembered being told he was found inside his Volkswagen in the desert. Cheryl did not remember if it was the FBI or police that told her Chester was having a sandwich and watching television at his apartment on base when he received a call from Lisbeth. Cheryl believed maybe Lisbeth called and told Chester that Patrick was missing, which would cause Chester to rush to their house to be murdered. She claimed she was told Roger hit Chester from behind and stabbed him more than twenty-seven times. Cheryl believed Roger and Lisbeth killed Chester but does not believe Patrick was involved. Cheryl believed Chester, who had been an Army Ranger, would have killed them had he not been attacked from behind.

Cheryl told Detective Arias that after Chester's death, Lisbeth told Cheryl she and Chester were working on reconciliation, but Cheryl told Lisbeth she knew that was a lie, that she had spoken to Chester two weeks before his death when he told her he wanted to divorce Lisbeth. Cheryl also said that about six months before

Chester's death, Lisbeth told her if anything happened to her, they should tell the police Chester had done it as he had beaten her in the past.

Cheryl recalled about one year after the murder, she bluffed Lisbeth by telling her a private investigator had re-opened Chester's case. Lisbeth immediately responded she did not want the case re-opened, but Cheryl countered her family wanted to find out who killed Chester. Lisbeth told Cheryl she was on her way to Cheryl's house. When Lisbeth arrived with Roger, Lisbeth asked what information the investigator was inquiring about. Cheryl continued her ruse by telling Lisbeth the fictitious investigator was asking questions about Lisbeth and about what the FBI had uncovered. Lisbeth emphatically told Cheryl the case was over and she did not want it re-opened. The two women continued to argue until Lisbeth told Cheryl whoever killed Chester might turn around and kill Cheryl and Cheryl's mother and son. Cheryl was alarmed by this threat and became very afraid of Lisbeth and Roger. Cheryl contacted FBI and advised them of Lisbeth's statements, but they told her they could do nothing about it. Cheryl told Detective Arias that was the last time she spoke to Lisbeth.

Cheryl Ellington said that a year or two before, Patrick Garrett had contacted her after many years of no communication. Patrick told Cheryl his mother Lisbeth had prevented him from contacting Cheryl or her sisters. He also told her of Roger's and Lisbeth's admissions to having killed Chester. Patrick swore to his aunt he had nothing to do with his father's death and he was waiting for his mother to pass away; then he would go to the authorities and turn in Roger. Patrick expressed to Cheryl he wanted to help put his brother in prison but all of the evidence was gone, and it would be difficult to prove. It seemed to her that Patrick was in no hurry to report the confessions to police. It had been more than a year since Patrick told his aunts about the admissions, and yet nothing had changed, and Chester's killers were still free to live their lives as if nothing had happened.

After an initially pleasant reunion between Patrick and his father's family, their relationship became stressed to the point that Cheryl and her sisters were no longer speaking to Patrick.

Cheryl concluded the interview by telling Detective Arias that around February 2006, she received a call on her cell phone.

When she answered, an unidentified female voice told her someone wanted to speak with her. The next thing Cheryl heard was a recording of the song "Hail to the Chief". This shook Cheryl to her core, as the last time she heard that song was at Chester's funeral. To date, Cheryl did not know who was behind this call.

After studying the case file and speaking with Chester Garrett's sisters, Tony Arias came to believe Patrick would be key in solving the case, although it was possible Patrick simply lied about the confessions to try to ingratiate himself with his father's kin. Now Patrick was on the outs with them, and along with Jackie's statement that he was no longer speaking about the confessions, Tony was concerned Patrick would not be forthcoming if contacted at that time. Tony knew he needed some tangible proof to show Patrick, like one of his email messages to Maureen pulled directly from Patrick's email account, so Patrick could not simply dismiss it as miscommunication. Therefore, Tony made every effort to find the email exchanges between Patrick and Maureen.

A few days later, Tony Arias received a compact disc containing a full snapshot of Patrick's e-mail account as a result of the Grand Jury Subpoena requests. Unfortunately, no records from Maureen's online account were available, as her provider did not maintain historical data due to the high volume of data.

Tony spent days going through Patrick's voluminous emails, but found no messages between Patrick and Maureen. Instead, he found emails between Patrick and a female friend in which Patrick claimed to have played football for the Dallas Cowboys, and others where he purported to be a Hollywood actor.

Even without emails referencing Lisbeth's and Roger's confessions, and knowing Patrick was avoiding the topic of confessions with the sisters, Tony felt it was time to directly contact Patrick. Tony proposed confronting Patrick at his Las Vegas home without warning, so as to not to allow Patrick an opportunity to avoid the detectives or formulate some story to throw them off. It was a risky move, as Patrick could simply shut the door in their faces or not even open it, resulting in a waste of time and money. Sergeant Belknap agreed to take the risk. Tony Arias and James Belknap had known each other since the 1980s when they worked uniform patrol together and both had a great deal of faith in the other's instincts and skill.

Chapter 48

On the afternoon of August 9, 2006, Detectives Tony Arias and Jim Reuter knocked on Patrick Garrett's door in Las Vegas, Nevada. There was no answer, so they sat in their rental car across the street and waited. At about 7:00pm, Patrick drove up to the house. They waited a few minutes, allowing Patrick to settle in before they approached. Tony rang the doorbell and knocked on the front door several times before Patrick answered. Tony identified himself as a detective with the El Paso Sheriff's Office. Patrick was obviously stunned. Tony asked him if they could step inside and speak with him. Patrick's eyes were opened wide, and his mouth hung open for several seconds until he managed to utter, "Yes, come in." Patrick was tall and heavy set, easily over 300 pounds. Until that moment, Tony still pictured Patrick in his mind as a twelve-year-old boy from 1977.

Detective Arias informed Patrick the Sheriff's Office had recently re-examined his father's case. Tony explained there had been new developments, and with advancements in science and technology such as DNA profiling, they believed they were now closer than ever to solving the murder. Patrick, still appearing somewhat stunned, stated he was told some of the evidence was lost. He added that around 1996, he had been interviewed by an El Paso Sheriff's County Detective, name forgotten, who had traveled to Neosho, Missouri, to talk to Patrick while Patrick was in jail on an "Interference with Child Custody" charge. This El Paso detective told Patrick he knew Lisbeth and Roger had killed his father. The detective offered Patrick a deal to drop the Missouri Interference with Custody charges if Patrick agreed to testify against his mother and brother in Texas.

According to Patrick, this El Paso detective told him the Sheriff's Office had lost the baseball bat used to kill his father as well as a section of wall that was part of their evidence. The detective also mentioned a dagger, part of a plaque awarded to Chester Garrett he suspected had been used in the murder. Patrick submitted to a voice analysis test by the detective, who explained this test would detect if Patrick was being deceitful. Patrick claimed he was not told if he passed or failed the test. Patrick said that after the test, he made it clear to the detective he would not agree to anything, and if the detective had such a strong case against his brother and mother, he should follow through and prosecute them without his participation or assistance.

Tony Arias explained to Patrick he did not know who had interviewed him in 1996, but he assured him the case evidence had not been compromised in any way and was safe in the Sheriff's Office evidence vault. This was a bluff by Detective Arias, as he did not know where Patrick's loyalties lay. Detective Arias could also see Patrick was on a fishing expedition, trying to feel out the detectives for information. Tony responded to Patrick's questions quickly and with total confidence to maintain an upper hand during their exchange. Seemingly satisfied, Patrick recounted his memory of the events that night his father was killed.

Patrick remembered going to either the 5:00pm or 7:00pm showing of the movie "Silver Streak" at Cielo Vista Mall with his friend Matthew "Buddy" Larson. Roger Garrett was supposed to pick them up, but he didn't show. Patrick recalled it was cold and dark outside. After fifteen or twenty minutes they called Buddy's parents for a ride. When they got to Buddy's house, a few houses down from the Garretts', Patrick walked home and found it dark. He rang the doorbell with no response. Patrick believed no one was home, so he sat and waited by the garage door for another fifteen to twenty minutes before walking back to Buddy's house. Patrick called home with no answer. After a while, he called again, and this time Roger answered. Patrick walked home and saw the porch light on. Roger met Patrick at the front door and sent him to bed without supper. Patrick did not see his mother that night or the following morning. Patrick went to school the next morning and learned later that day his father's body had been found. Roger picked up Patrick at school, and when they got home, two military officers were speaking to their mother. Patrick also remembered going with his family to Thomason General Hospital to see his father's body.

Patrick said he had always believed his mother, Lisbeth Garrett, and his brother, Roger Garrett, killed his father. Whenever Patrick spoke of the murder to either of them, it was "like taboo";

they refused to talk about it. Patrick remembers his parents were separated but was not aware they were in the process of divorce. He now believed his mother and brother killed his father before the divorce was finalized, because divorce would leave them without income. Shortly after his father died, his mother purchased a new home.

      Patrick said his father was hard on Roger, and he recalled one time when his father was hitting his mother and Roger had to intervene to get his father off their mother. Patrick also remembered after his father's death, police found blood in the driveway and garage of their home. Patrick explained the blood came from a friend named Frank Smith, now deceased, who had a nosebleed after getting hit during a basketball game.

      Patrick told the detectives that while he occasionally called his mother, he had not seen her in about ten years, and had not spoken to Roger in about five years. In closing, Detective Arias urged Patrick to contact him if he recalled or learned any other information, and they left.

      Tony Arias had chosen beforehand to not disclose to Patrick he was in contact with his aunts and was aware of the confessions made to Patrick by Roger and Lisbeth. It's best to not educate a witness any more than necessary during an investigation. Tony wanted Patrick to stew for a while and decide on his own to willingly cooperate with law enforcement. Tony gambled that this meeting would push Patrick off the fence and prompt him to be forthcoming in the future; to feel that Tony was giving him an invitation to choose the right team, and make the correct moral decision. Tony felt Patrick was the most critical witness in this case, and he didn't want to ruin what rapport they had just established by trying to force information from him. Tony was willing to wait.

      Tony Arias also had to figure out who this El Paso detective was who had gone to Missouri and interviewed Patrick in jail in 1996. This new information caught him by surprise. Tony later discovered that El Paso Sheriff's Department Captain Gary Gabbert signed out the original paper Garrett case file in 1995. Captain Gabbert was in charge of EPSD CID at the time and apparently initiated work on the CAP case. Unfortunately, no reports in the electronic case file indicated a trip to Missouri, an interview of Patrick Garrett, or that Captain Gabbert was ever involved with the case. Since the logbook showed that Captain Gabbert signed out the file in 1995 but never signed it back in, Tony could only conclude that Captain Gabbert did not return it. EPSO Detective Jim Reuter tracked down Captain Gabbert and ironically discovered that after retiring from EPSD, Gabbert moved to Missouri and became a rural county sheriff. However, in 2006, Gary Gabbert was unable to recall what he did with the file or where it might currently be.

Chapter 49

Five years later, on May 5, 2011, Detectives Tony Arias and Jerome Washington interviewed Lieutenant Colonel (Ret) Harrell Glenn Hall, Chester Garrett's Commanding Officer at Fort Bliss when he was killed. The detectives were happy to note that LTC Hall's recollections closely matched his original statements given 34 years before.

LTC Hall said when he took command of the Student Battalion at Fort Bliss in 1975, MAJ Garrett was already the Executive Officer for the Battalion. LTC Hall said MAJ Garrett was one of the highest decorated officers in the United States Army at that time, as LTC Hall did not believe there were any Medal of Honor recipients currently alive (the Medal of Honor being the only major award Garrett was not awarded). LTC Hall said Garrett received the Distinguished Service Cross, the Silver Star and five Bronze Stars for Valor in Vietnam. LTC Hall described Garrett as 6'3" tall and weighing 235 pounds, a former professional ballplayer who was in "magnificent physical condition."

LTC Hall was aware MAJ Garrett and his wife were living apart. LTC Hall was unable to recall where he heard Mrs. Garrett would "lurk" in the BOQ parking lot with her two boys, trying to catch the Major taking a woman into his BOQ to show the boys what kind of man their father was.

LTC Hall said he had always felt MAJ Garrett's wife was responsible for his murder. He recalled they were in the process of a divorce, which he thought was close to being finalized.

LTC Hall said he had the "very agonizing experience" of having to inform Mrs. Garrett of the Major's death. LTC Hall again recalled how Mrs. Garrett and her eldest son Roger were dressed in matching terrycloth robes. LTC Hall said after a few minutes Mrs. Garrett worked up a sort of a cry, but to him, Mrs. Garrett's reaction to the news of the Major's death did not seem genuine.

LTC Hall first learned of the murder from his Brigade Commander, who said a car with license plates registered to MAJ

Garrett had been found with a body inside. LTC Hall recalled having to identify Garrett's body at the morgue. LTC Hall also recalled being told there were tennis shoe tracks by the car, and he saw one of the boys wearing tennis shoes when the family came to the hospital. LTC Hall said when a search warrant was conducted there were no tennis shoes to be found in the house. LTC Hall did not recall how he got this information, but that was his impression. LTC Hall said he was told by an investigator the garage floor was washed with some kind of acid.

LTC Hall said he last spoke to MAJ Garrett the day before his body was found. LTC Hall remembered MAJ Garrett and his wife visiting his home for a Battalion Officers function.

LTC Hall gave the eulogy at MAJ Garrett's funeral, and said although it was an honor to do so, it was also one of the most painful experiences he has ever had.

LTC Hall concluded the interview by saying there were a lot of Vietnam soldiers at the time who thought smoking marijuana was fine, but he and MAJ Garrett opposed it. He added he was the one who administered Article 15 punishments for this, not MAJ Garrett, so he couldn't think of anyone in the battalion having any issue with MAJ Garrett for that.

Chapter 50

1349 Backus Street, 2018

Detective Arias consulted with DPS Analyst Ceniceros about the probability of obtaining useable evidence from the garage at 1349 Backus. Ms. Ceniceros advised it was highly unlikely any type of DNA could be extracted after so much time had elapsed since the murder. Regardless, Sergeant Belknap and Detective Arias approached the current owner of the Backus residence for permission to process the garage for evidence, particularly in areas where detectives had observed what they believed to be blood in 1977.

On January 5, 2012, 35 years and two days after Chester Garrett's murder, the garage at 1349 Backus was processed by EPSO Crime Records Evidence and Forensic Section technicians. A Luminol Processing Technique, used to enhance latent blood stains, was applied to the garage. Sketches of the garage and a projection sketch of the south wall of the garage were also completed.

In 1977, detectives observed blood spatter on the south wall of the garage. An area of sheetrock was cut out by Detective Chuy Reyes, and submitted into evidence. That portion of the wall was now covered with wood paneling. The current owner of the residence allowed crime scene technicians to remove the wood paneling, and they discovered the original hole where the sheetrock was cut out in 1977. It had not been repaired. This allowed technicians to swab along the edges of the cut-out area. Once processing was complete, collected swabs were submitted into evidence and subsequently sent to the DPS lab for analysis.

Results of the DPS analysis showed no DNA profile matches were obtained or no blood was detected. It is important to note that in 1977, DNA science was non-existent, so blood sent to the FBI lab could only be tested for blood type or group, such as A-Positive, B-Negative, etc.

One piece of evidence that was a red flag for Tony Arias was a man's blue jacket found lying on MAJ Garrett's body inside his Volkswagen. Because it was resting on top of his body, it had to have been put there by the killer after the body was placed inside the Volkswagen. The jacket did not belong to MAJ Garrett as it was a size "medium." On the other hand, it could have fit Roger Garrett. In 1977, the jacket was sent to the FBI lab with negative results for blood or hairs. In 2013, Detective Arias submitted the jacket to the DPS lab to check for wearer DNA, requesting particular attention to areas typically in contact with the wearer's skin, particularly the wrists and collar. Unfortunately, no DNA profile was found.

During the years Tony Arias worked the Garrett investigation, he also carried his usual heavy caseload, punctuated with high profile cases involving capital murder and kidnapping. His plate was full, but he grew obsessed with Chester Garrett's murder and felt strongly that he owed it to Jackie and her family to continue. Throughout the years, he spoke to Jackie every three or four months. He advised her of his progress but had to keep it brief to maintain case integrity. Sensitive case details have no place in public purview.

Chapter 51

On January 3, 2013, Patrick Garrett left a voicemail on the published telephone number for EPSO CAP. He identified himself, said he was in El Paso at the Colonia Motor Hotel on Dyer Street, and said he had information about MAJ Garrett's murder. No one intercepted this message until some days later due to the detectives' holiday schedule and miscommunication.

On January 5, 2013, Sergeant Belknap received an e-mail and forwarded it to Detective Arias. It was dated the day before, and it was from Patrick Garrett. The email contained the following message:

"Hello,

My name is Patrick Garrett. My father was Chester Garrett, who was murdered Jan. 4th, 1977. I am not sure if you were one of the men who came to talk with me in Las Vegas, NV, a few years ago, but I need to speak with you if you are the person who is still looking into this cold case. I have details that will solve the case, and I need to speak with someone. I am staying at the Colonia Motel.

I have left several messages with the CID # given to me from the dispatcher, but I have not received a call back from anyone. Please, I need your help as my mother, who is also in this room, heard me call the Sheriff's office...I thought she was asleep; she was not. She then got up and used her cell to call my brother. I could not hear everything that was said, but I did hear her tell him she plans on buying a gun.

I do not know what else to do, I have no job, and I have no car. I am trying to get back on my feet, and I have nowhere else to go. Please contact me as soon as possible. I fear my mother and brother are plotting to silence me somehow.

Please call me asap.
Pat"

Tony Arias called Detective Jerome Washington and asked him to meet Tony at the Colonia Motor Hotel on Dyer St. in northeast El Paso.

They arrived and went into the motel office. As they spoke with the clerk, Patrick suddenly walked into the office. He appeared tired and disheveled but seemed relieved the detectives had finally arrived to meet him. Tony told Patrick he was the detective Patrick had met in Las Vegas, and he had received and read Patrick's email. Patrick said he was ready to provide information that would solve his father's murder. He said he was staying at this hotel with his mother, Lisbeth Garrett, and explained he had come to El Paso to help clean out his mother's house on Gallic Court. Patrick added his mother was being forced out of the home by Adult Protective Services because it was "uninhabitable." Patrick agreed to accompany the detectives to the Sheriff's Office.

On the drive to headquarters, Tony assured Patrick he was doing the right thing and asked Patrick why it had taken so long for him to come forward. Patrick explained when he first spoke to Tony in Las Vegas, he was protecting his family and did not want to hurt them. He said he lost a son in 2009, and in the process he lost his faith. In 2010 he found Christianity and now wanted justice for his father.

Once at headquarters, Patrick wrote the following statement:

> "On January 5th, 2013, I came to the El Paso Sheriff's Office to say what happened to my father. I wanted to say what happened, because it's the right thing to do. In between December 25th, 1990 to January 1st, 1991, I was getting ready to move to Missouri. I was at my mother's house on Gallic Court here in El Paso. My brother Roger Garrett and I were sitting on the front porch. We were talking about the Gulf War and how I was thinking about enlisting in the military. We started talking about my father Major Chester Garrett, and I asked him if there was anything he wanted to tell me.
>
> "Roger put his head down and his arm around

my shoulder. Roger said, 'I need to get this off my chest.' He said he and my mother Lisbeth Garrett killed dad. He said they lured Dad over to Backus St, where we lived, to fix a broken dishwasher. When Dad looked inside the dishwasher, he was on his knees. Roger said he hit Dad on the back of the head with a baseball bat. After that, Mom took a dagger that was on a plaque that was given to Dad from his unit during the war. It was a black dagger about six inches. Roger said Mom stabbed Dad several times. I don't know how many; he didn't say.

"After that, they dragged him to the garage. Roger said dad was still moaning and gurgling, so mom hit him over the head with a baseball bat. They put him into the back seat of his Volkswagen Beetle and left the house. Roger said dad was wearing a sweat suit that Roger and I had given him for Christmas. It was a red, white and blue sweat suit. Mom followed Roger in the Mercury. They drove him out to Avenues of Americas. He said there was a dump out there. They left dad in the back seat of the Beetle and went back home.

"I don't remember the exact night this happened. I just remember it was a school night. My mom had given me money to go to the movies with Buddy Larson. It wasn't normal, because I wouldn't be allowed to go out, because it was a school night. My mom dropped Buddy and me off at the movies at Cielo Vista Mall. I remember the movie was "Silver Streak."

"I still to this day can't watch that movie because it reminded me of when my dad was killed. When the movie was over, my mom was supposed to pick us up, but she never did. Buddy called his mom, who picked us up. We went back to Buddy's house which was right down the street from mine. I walked home and didn't see any lights on. I knocked on the door and rang the doorbell, and no one answered. I went back to Buddy's house and used his telephone to call my house, but no one answered.

"Buddy's garage to his house had been converted

to a game room. We played a game of pool, and I could see my house from there. Later, I saw the porch light on at my house, so I went home. When I got home, I knocked, and Roger answered the door immediately. He said for me to go to bed right away. He wouldn't let me go around the house. He physically walked me to my room. When I woke up, Roger gave me a bowl of cereal in my bedroom. It was unusual for that because we always ate in the kitchen. Roger told me I had to go to school right away and made me go out the front door. That was also weird because my routine was to go through the garage to get out. Roger wouldn't let me go into the kitchen. So, I walked to school after that.

"Roger picked me up after school and wouldn't let any of my friends go with me. Roger said Dad was in an accident and died. When I got home, there was a military officer and a military chaplain there. They told me my father was not coming home again, and that he had passed away. I remember people coming by the house, bringing food.

"Roger told me that night dad was late coming to the house to fix the dishwasher. Therefore, they didn't have time to clean up after they killed him. My mom was supposed to pick me up from the movies but didn't because dad showed up at the house late. Roger said after I went to sleep that night, they put all their clothes and shoes into black plastic bags. He said one of the trash bags also had the dagger. He said they went to different 7-Eleven stores on the Westside of El Paso and dumped the trash bags into separate dumpsters.

"Roger said Mom would buy him a car if he helped her. Roger said Mom didn't want a divorce from Dad because she didn't have anything. He said Dad had a life insurance policy that was worth a lot of money. I remember my mom used to sit outside his quarters on Ft. Bliss and watch him, thinking he was cheating on her.

"My mom had told me I had to clean the garage floor. She had acid that you could buy at the Cashway, a local hardware store. She had a gallon bucket full of water. I had to wear dishwashing gloves and had a scrub brush. Roger and I poured water down on the floor and then poured the acid on it. Roger and I would scrub the floor with the brush, and then wash the floor down with the water hose.

"As you are facing the garage, I had to clean the floor on the left side. There was a red tint on the floor that went from the kitchen to about halfway into the garage. It was about two and half feet wide. That is what we had to clean up. I also had to clean the wall on the left side of the garage. I didn't use acid on that. I used 409 cleaner and scrubbed it off, but I didn't get it all. That portion of the wall I had to clean was about 1 ½ to 2 feet from the floor up. I remember the Sheriff's took that piece of the wall off as evidence. When we were done, we washed the garage floor down with the water hose. We didn't know it until afterward, but it turned the floor white, and it went down the street about five houses. I remember our neighbor John Wentzel was mad because it turned the curb in front of his house white. It also turned one side of our driveway white. Later, Roger and I went back with acid and turned the other half of the driveway white so it would match.

"Around the same time, I had chores to do. I had to dust all the wood in the family room, where the fireplace was. My dad had the plaque with the dagger above the fireplace. When I was cleaning the wood, I noticed the dagger was gone.

"The investigation had started, and there was going to be a Grand Jury hearing. My mom didn't want me to testify. She told me to say that I didn't go to the movies, but then she realized I was going to say it. Then she said to say Roger forgot to pick me up, because he was helping his friend Robert Snelson study. She also told me not to say when I came home that night, no one was there. Mom would say 'If anybody asks' whenever we talked about my dad. I remember before the investigation started, Mom changed the tires to her car. She told me she had bought Goodyear tires, and that her friend Otis Bell in Fort Worth got her a good deal. I knew the tires were new because I remember seeing a white tag on one of the tires that hadn't been taken off. Mom also bought her and Roger new shoes. She didn't buy me any. I remember Mom buying Roger a Fiat after this and then another car when that one broke down. I also remember the life insurance company giving my mother a check. After the man left, Mom and Roger went into the kitchen, and they were laughing.

"Back in September of 2010, I was in Lafayette, Louisiana, living at Roger's house with my mom too. Around that time, I had become a Christian, and I had asked Roger if he worried about losing his soul because of what he and Mom had done. He told me he prayed for forgiveness and thought he had been forgiven. I told him the Bible said he needed to confess from the mouth to be forgiven. He proceeded to tell me the same thing he did in 1990. I told him I wasn't a pastor, and he needed to confess to the police. He didn't say anything.

"I needed to clear my conscience as well, so on December 23rd of 2012, I called the Sheriff's Office to talk to someone on the case. My mom heard me on the phone and immediately called Roger. I heard her saying she was looking to buy a gun. Mom gave me the phone and Roger started cussing at me. I told him I had to do it. He said he was calling my bluff. After that I started having problems with my mom. She has been accusing me of stealing from her and pushing her down.

"Anytime I ever asked my mom about what happened, she always said she didn't remember that part of her life. She also said she never re-married because she didn't want to lose any benefits from my dad. I was about 14 or 15, and my friends would ask about what happened to my dad. I asked my mom, and she would tell me to tell people I didn't remember that part of my life.

"Back in 2006, Sheriff's Detectives had come to see me in Las Vegas. I didn't tell them what Roger had told me because I didn't want to hurt my family. In June of 2009, I lost my son. I lost my faith after that, and I blamed God. I met a man in downtown Reno who gave me advice about good and evil. It later led me to Christianity in 2010. Since then I have been struggling with this. I want justice for my father. If I don't come clean, I am just as guilty for not saying anything. I'm not looking for money. I just want to get this off my chest and get on with my life."

Patrick's statement put EPSO CAP into high gear. Finally they had some workable evidence. It was now essential to corroborate as much of his information as possible. Sergeant Belknap's crew prepared a list of people to interview and divvied-up a list of tasks and items to further research.

Tony Arias was nagged by the missing paper case file and Captain Gary Gabbert's undocumented investigative efforts in the mid-1990s. Now that Patrick had come forward and they had a real shot at prosecuting the murderers, they needed the original file more than ever. It bothered Tony enough that Sergeant Belknap ordered a stand down and exhaustive search of anywhere in the Sheriff's Office complex the missing file might be hiding. After a few frustrating days they hit pay dirt. Sure enough, the original accordion file was discovered in the file room after all, misfiled inside another larger file. And to Tony's delight, Captain Gabbert had in fact filed several reports about his activities, although he had not filed those same reports electronically, which would have been the norm for 1995.

On January 9, 2013, EPSO Detective Jerome Washington met with Lisbeth Garrett's Adult Protective Services (APS) caseworker. APS filed a report of "Physical Self Neglect" on September 16, 2010, due to the dilapidated state of the residence on Gallic Court, and initiated removal proceedings against Lisbeth on December 31, 2012. According to the caseworker, the house had become unlivable due to rodents and excessive hoarding by Lisbeth. The kitchen was so full of trash and debris it was impossible to enter. Lisbeth told the caseworker her son Patrick had come to El Paso to clean the house, and they planned to move into the residence together. Lisbeth complained to the caseworker that Patrick accused her of killing his father, but claimed the allegations were not true.

The caseworker also informed Detective Washington she planned to contact Lisbeth's other son, Roger Garrett, who currently resided in Knoxville, Tennessee, to see if he was able to care for her.

While Detective Washington interviewed the APS caseworker, Sergeant Belknap and Detective Arias obtained a copy of movie listings for January 3, 1977, from El Paso Times newspaper archives. The movie "Silver Streak" was, in fact, shown that day at Cielo Vista Mall Cinemas at 1:30, 3:30, 5:30, 7:35 and 9:30, corroborating Patrick's statement.

On January 14, 2013, Detective Jorge Andrade interviewed Mathew "Buddy" Larson, Patrick's childhood friend and neighbor. Buddy Larson said although he was very good friends with Patrick, and they spent a great deal of time together, he did not specifically recall going to the movies with Patrick on that school night to see the movie "Silver Streak." He did, however, recall an incident when he and Patrick were riding with Patrick's mother to school one morning, when Lisbeth Garrett suddenly pulled over and stopped, and ordered Patrick to get out and beat up a boy who was walking on the sidewalk. Patrick, like a robot, did exactly what his mother told him and beat the smaller child. After pummeling the boy for a while, Mrs. Garrett yelled to Patrick to stop and get back in the car. Patrick immediately stopped the assault and got into the car, and Mrs. Garrett drove the boys to school. Buddy Larson later found out this boy who was assaulted had said some bad things about Mrs. Garrett, so she had Patrick teach this boy a lesson.

Chapter 52

On January 17, 2013, Sergeant James Belknap and Detective Tony Arias traveled to Neosho, Missouri, to interview Jeanne Patterson and her sister, Patricia Loveland. Jeanne was Patrick Garrett's former wife. Both ladies were eager to cooperate with the investigators.

Jeanne Patterson said Patrick told her about his father's death when they began dating. After they were married in September 1990, Patrick shared his perspective of his father's murder with her and said he had a lot of unanswered questions. Jeanne said Patrick was only twelve or thirteen when his father died and thought what he recalled from that night didn't coincide with what he heard growing up.

Jeanne said that in December 1990, she and Patrick were staying at Lisbeth Garrett's home on Gallic Court in El Paso. Patrick's brother, Roger Garrett, was also staying at Lisbeth's home. According to Jeanne, Patrick was determined to find out any information related to his father's murder, and she recalled accompanying Patrick to the library to research newspaper archives about it.

On a weeknight before Christmas, Jeanne, Patrick, and Roger were sitting in the den of the Gallic Court home. Patrick questioned Roger about the murder, no accusations, just questions related to Chester's death. Patrick told Roger, "I have questions about it; I've been wondering a long time." At first Roger was reluctant to talk, but he told Patrick someday he would tell Patrick what he needed to know. Jeanne described the tension in the room as being high.

Jeanne said Lisbeth Garrett arrived home later that evening. When she learned Patrick and Roger had discussed the murder, she became incensed and the three began to argue. Jeanne wanted no part of this conversation. She heard Lisbeth say, "It looks like I raised a bunch of idiots." Roger's retort to Lisbeth was, "You haven't; all you know how to raise is killers", and he stormed out of the room. Patrick followed him, and they both went outside to the front porch. Lisbeth went upstairs while Jeanne hid in the bathroom to avoid any confrontation with Lisbeth. The bathroom had a window that opened into the garage.

After a while, Lisbeth came downstairs and went into the garage. Jeanne watched through the window as Lisbeth stood in the dark next to the garage door, obviously nervous, trying to hear what Roger and Patrick were discussing. They remained outside for quite a while, so Jeanne went to bed.

When Patrick went to bed, he was emotionally upset. He had tears in his eyes and told Jeanne, "Roger and my mom killed my father." Patrick went on to say Roger explained to him that Lisbeth had worked on Roger mentally for months before the murder, convincing Roger that Chester was a bad person and was going to do bad things and leave them. Lisbeth also told Roger that Chester was threatening to take the boys to his new assignment, so Lisbeth and Roger planned to kill Chester. Roger's part was to have a baseball bat ready, and they placed knives on a dish towel as if they were drying them. They planned a ruse to lure Chester to the house to check on the broken dishwasher.

Jeanne said Patrick told her that night that Roger told him after Chester arrived, he bent down to inspect the dishwasher and Roger smashed him in the head with the bat. Chester fell to the floor, delirious from the blow to the head and asked, "Why are you doing this to me?" Roger and Lisbeth grabbed the knives and stabbed Chester over and over. Roger drove Chester's Volkswagen into the garage, and they dragged Chester to the garage and into the back seat of the Volkswagen. They drove him to a secluded area outside of town. Once they disposed of Chester, they got rid of the knives in a dumpster in south El Paso. Lisbeth bought new tires for her car and bought new shoes for Roger to cover their tracks.

Patrick was at the movies with a friend when his dad died. Jeanne said Patrick often questioned why he was allowed to go to a movie on a school night. When Patrick got home from the movies, the house was dark and locked. Nobody answered when he rang the doorbell. Patrick sat on the driveway leaning against the garage for a few minutes and then walked to his friend's house, a few doors down on the same street. When Patrick got to his friend's home, he called his house phone, and either Lisbeth or Roger answered and told him to come home. Patrick thought it was strange in the short time it took him to get to his friend's house he didn't see a car pull into his driveway. Patrick didn't believe there was sufficient time for Roger and Lisbeth to drive into the garage, pull down the garage door, go inside the home and answer his call. Jeanne said Patrick told her it seemed to him that Roger or Lisbeth, or both, were home, but did not open the door when he rang the doorbell.

Jeanne said Patrick told her he saw Roger wearing new shoes and there were new white wall tires on his mother's car the day he found out about his father's death. Patrick also told her Roger and Lisbeth began having long private talks in Lisbeth's room with the door shut. Patrick also noticed a dagger from his father's knife collection was now gone.

Jeanne recalled Patrick telling her Lisbeth "fought" to prevent law enforcement officials from interviewing him because he was "emotionally fragile" and had Patrick see a psychologist.

Jeanne also remembered speaking with Roger Garrett's second wife, Terry Heffelfinger in El Paso around 1996. Jeanne's sister, Patricia Loveland, was present. Terry was visibly frightened as she confided in Jeanne and Patricia that Roger had admitted to Terry that he and his mother had killed his father.

Sergeant Belknap and Detective Arias next interviewed Jeanne Patterson's sister, Patricia Loveland. Patricia said that in the summer of 1991, Patrick Garrett told her that his brother Roger admitted to Patrick the previous December that he and his mother, "Liz" Garrett, had murdered his father, Chester Garrett.

Patricia told the detectives that Patrick explained to her how Lisbeth and Roger committed the attack, and she repeated Jeanne's description of the ruse of repairing the dishwasher. Patrick also told Patricia Loveland he had gone to a movie that night with a friend and could not get into the house when he got home. He told Patricia it was not typical for his mother to let him go out with friends on a school night.

Patricia repeated what Jeanne had told the detectives about Roger's ex-wife, Terry Heffelfinger: that she and Jeanne Patterson both spoke with Terry about the murder. Patricia said Terry was visibly frightened as she talked about Roger and the murder of Chester. Terry told them Roger also admitted to her that he and his mother killed Chester Garrett.

Chapter 53

In El Paso, on January 23, 2013, Detectives Tony Arias and Jorge Andrade met with Theresa Heffelfinger, Roger Garrett's second wife. Tony explained to Ms. Heffelfinger they were investigating Chester Garrett's murder, and she replied, "Oh...his step-father. Why, what did Mr. Garrett do again?" and laughed nervously. Tony explained the Sheriff's Office had re-opened the case in 2006 and were re-interviewing witnesses.

Theresa Heffelfinger said she recalled being interviewed by Captain Gabbert of the Sheriff's Office in 1995 regarding this case. Theresa said when she saw Tony's business card on her door, from a previous attempt to contact her, she figured it had to do with Roger and thought he had gotten into trouble again.

Theresa Heffelfinger told the detectives she had a gut feeling she should not have married Roger, but he was very good at "acting" and would "tell you what you wanted to hear." Theresa described herself as "very spiritual" and believed the universe has a way of righting a person's wrongs, so, once they divorced, Roger was removed from her life.

Theresa Heffelfinger said she married Roger Garrett in April 1992, and divorced him on December 17, 1993. She specifically recalls the date of her divorce as she and her friends celebrated by throwing a divorce party. Theresa mentioned numerous reasons for her divorce from Roger; his drinking, cocaine use, lying, running up credit card bills, and Roger's fundamental interest in climbing the corporate ladder at his job with Hinckley and Schmidt.

Theresa Heffelfinger said that about four months into the marriage, in about August of 1992, Roger confessed to her he and his mother killed his father, Chester Garrett. According to Theresa, Roger's story was Lisbeth "presented to him under pretense" reasons to convince Roger to help her kill his father, including that Chester posed a threat to her life. Theresa said she asked Roger if some part of him at any time said, "I'm not going to do it", and he replied his mother thoroughly convinced him her life was in danger, so he did it.

Roger described to Theresa how his mother was very methodical on how they carried out the crime and how they covered it afterward. Roger also said Lisbeth got the idea from a television show called "The Perfect Murder". Roger told Theresa he believed District Attorney Steve Simmons targeted him for his cocaine arrest and long probation because they couldn't get him for the murder. Theresa told the detectives she asked Roger during the same conversation if he would ever kill someone again, and he replied he would not.

Theresa Heffelfinger related how Roger tried to kidnap his daughter Sabrina from his first wife, Katherine Devaney, who was Native American and lived on a reservation near Farmington, New Mexico. Katherine firmly believed the kidnapping was instigated by Lisbeth Garrett. Theresa said Patrick went to jail in Missouri for kidnapping his children too, and she believed Lisbeth was behind that crime as well.

Tony Arias asked Theresa Heffelfinger if she could provide names of any of Roger's friends or anyone else who might have information about Roger. She gave him the name of Debbie Drake, who she said introduced her to Roger Garrett.

Chapter 54

On January 25, 2013, Tony Arias contacted Jennifer Molina, MAJ Garrett's girlfriend in 1976, when she was a private in the U.S. Army. It was clear to Tony even after all these years she still had a strong emotional attachment to Chester Garrett. Jennifer said to this day she still remembered him on his birthday. She recalled being assaulted with an iron by Lisbeth Garrett in 1976.

On January 26, 2013, Tony Arias contacted Richard Eugene Magruder, who worked directly for MAJ Chester Garrett as a clerk at Battalion Headquarters at Fort Bliss. Magruder confirmed his dates of service at Fort Bliss from early 1975 to June 1976, when he was transferred to Korea. Magruder said he was in Korea when he found out about MAJ Garrett's death.

Magruder described MAJ Garrett as the "greatest warrior" he ever met, who "lived his life that way." He said MAJ Garrett was 5'11", 220 pounds, ran four miles each morning, didn't drink or smoke, "all military", and before the army he had pitched for the Chicago Cubs in the minor leagues. Magruder described MAJ Garrett as a fair man and a very caring individual, "a great guy, the real deal as far as a soldier." Magruder said he and MAJ Garrett were friends on duty and off duty. He knew about MAJ Garrett's girlfriend, Jennifer, and he knew MAJ Garrett was "on the outs" with his wife. Magruder speculated aloud if perhaps Mrs. Garrett had found out about MAJ Garrett's girlfriend Jennifer, and had him "set up" or maybe his kids were involved in drugs in a way that led to the Major's death. Magruder often answered the Major's phone when Mrs. Garrett called, and was routinely present when MAJ Garret argued with his wife on the telephone. According to Magruder, Mrs. Garrett was "spiteful", had a "very nasty disposition" and seemed perpetually "pissed off." If Magruder answered her calls to the office and told Mrs. Garrett the Major was not in his office "it was like you were lying to her." Magruder remembered telling Jennifer Molina the Major was still married, and added that Mrs. Garrett "was pretty much a bitch". Magruder concluded the interview by stating his best guess was that MAJ Garrett's family was involved in his murder.

Sergeant Belknap and Detective Arias had a series of meetings with El Paso County Assistant District Attorneys (ADAs) Denise Butterworth and Kyle Myers to discern if there was sufficient probable cause to obtain arrest warrants for Roger Garrett and Lisbeth Garrett for 1st Degree Murder. Tony Arias and CAP drafted a Probable Cause Affidavit which was ultimately revised into Arrest Affidavits for Lisbeth and Roger. It reads as follows:

> "On January 4, 1977, at approximately 9:32 AM, John Banuelos found the body of Major Chester Garrett, age 35, abandoned in the rear seat of his 1972 Volkswagen, three miles north of Interstate 10 on Avenue of the Americas in El Paso County, Texas. Garrett was dressed in a blue jogging suit and tennis shoes.
>
> "An autopsy was performed on the body of Major Garrett, and it revealed blunt injury fracture of the skull with severe contusions of the brain and numerous stab wounds.
>
> "Affidavits were obtained from Mrs. Lisbeth Garrett, wife of Chester Garrett, and Roger Garrett, step-son of MAJ Garret. They both indicated to El Paso Sheriff's investigators that MAJ Garrett had been at their home, 1349 Backus in El Paso, arriving at around 7:15 PM and leaving at about 8:20 PM the night of January 3, 1977. He was dressed in the same blue jogging suit he was found in the next day. A 'Consent to Search' was signed by Lisbeth Garrett, allowing Sheriff's detectives to search her residence and vehicle.
>
> "On January 13, 1977, EPSD Sergeant Timmons along with other Sheriff's officers arrived at 1349 Backus to search. Among the items they found was a bottle of Muriatic Acid that appeared to have been used to clean the garage floor on one side of a double car garage, along with what visually seemed to be blood spots on a sheetrock wall, in the garage.
>
> "During the investigation, EPSD investigators interviewed MAJ Garret's Commanding Officer, LTC

Harrell Hall, who advised that MAJ Garrett had been separated from Mrs. Garrett and was residing in Bachelor Officer Quarters (BOQ) at Fort Bliss, Texas.

"On January 5, 2013, Patrick Kevin Garrett met with El Paso Sheriff's Office (EPSO) Detectives, Antonio Arias and Jerome Washington. Patrick was twelve years of age when his father Chester Garret was murdered on January 3, 1977. Patrick provided a written statement with the following information:

"Patrick said that sometime between December 1990 and January 1, 1991, his brother, Roger Garrett, admitted to him that he (Roger) along with their mother, Lisbeth Anne Garrett, had killed their father, Chester Garrett, in the kitchen of their home, 1349 Backus, El Paso, Texas. Roger admitted to hitting Chester Garrett in the back of the head with a baseball bat and that their mother, Lisbeth, had stabbed Chester several times with a knife. Roger and Lisbeth dragged Chester from the kitchen into the garage where they placed his body into the back seat of his Volkswagen. They drove the Volkswagen to a dump around Avenue of the Americas where they left the Volkswagen with Chester inside. Roger and Lisbeth drove home in Lisbeth's vehicle.

"Patrick recalls that on the evening of January 3, 1977, his mother gave him money to go to the movies with a friend. This was highly unusual as it was a school night (Monday night). Patrick recalls going to the movie that evening with a friend. They were dropped off by Lisbeth Garrett at Cielo Vista Mall to watch the movie "Silver Streak" and were to be picked up by Lisbeth when the movie was over. Patrick recalls that neither his mother nor Roger showed up to pick them up and were subsequently picked up by his friend's parents. After arriving at his friend's home, Patrick walked home, but when he arrived the lights were off, and no one was home. Patrick walked back to his friend's home and waited until he saw a porch light go on at his house. When Patrick got home, he was physically escorted to his room by Roger, who told him to go to bed right away. The next morning Roger gave Patrick a bowl of cereal to eat in his bedroom and was not allowed to eat in the kitchen or to exit through the garage, as he usually did when he left for school. Patrick said Roger made him walk out the front door of the home. Later that day Patrick learned of his father's murder.

"Patrick also indicates in his statement that after his father's murder he helped his brother Roger clean the garage floor with acid. The cleanup was done under the direction of their mother, Lisbeth Garrett. Patrick indicates there was a red tint on the garage floor that was cleaned off by the acid. After cleaning the garage floor with the acid, it was washed down with the water hose. This caused the garage floor and driveway to turn white. The runoff went down the street about five houses.

"Patrick indicates in his written statement that in September of 2010, he was living with his brother Roger Garrett in Lafayette, Louisiana, when Roger again admitted to him that he (Roger) along with their mother, Lisbeth, had killed their father, Chester Garrett.

"A written statement was provided to EPSO by C. Jeanne Patterson on January 17, 2013. Ms. Patterson is the former wife of Patrick Garrett. In her statement, Ms. Patterson indicates that in December of 1990, Patrick told her that Roger had just admitted to him that he along with their mother had killed their father.

"Patricia Brock Loveland, in a written statement, said that in the summer of 1991, Patrick Garrett, her brother-in-law, told her that his brother, Roger Garrett, had admitted to him that he (Roger) along with their mother, Lisbeth Garrett, had murdered their father, Chester Garrett in 1977.

"Theresa Heffelfinger, the former wife of Roger Garrett, gave a written statement indicating that sometime around August 1992, Roger admitted to her that he along with his mother, Lisbeth Garrett, killed his step-father, Chester Garrett."

Chapter 55

On February 1, 2013, Detectives Jorge Andrade and Tony Arias met with a District Judge who signed both affidavits and issued Arrest Warrants for Roger Garrett and Lisbeth Garrett. Tony requested a search for Roger Garrett through the law enforcement support center and determined Roger was currently residing in the city of Knoxville, Tennessee. Tony contacted the Knoxville Police Department, who agreed to assist in locating and arresting Roger. EPSO CAP devised a plan to arrest Roger Garrett in Knoxville first and then arrest Lisbeth immediately after in El Paso.

On February 7, 2013, Detectives Arias and Andrade traveled to Knoxville, Tennessee. Upon arrival they met officers from Knoxville Police Department (KPD) at their headquarters to plan Roger's arrest. Being on KPD's home turf, the El Paso detectives let KPD take the lead in Roger's arrest operation and coordinated a safe plan agreeable to both agencies.

The team left KPD headquarters and drove to Roger's apartment on Arbor Trace Drive. Rain began to fall. KPD Sergeant Christopher Bell knocked on the door. It was answered by a woman who identified herself as Susan Garrett, Roger's wife. Sergeant Bell asked for Roger Garrett, and Mrs. Garrett replied her husband was not home, and was in fact at a job interview in Asheville, North Carolina. Mrs. Garrett said Roger had left early that morning, and she did not know if he would return home later this day or the next day. Sergeant Bell explained to Mrs. Garrett he needed to discuss a pending matter with Roger and asked for his cell phone number. Mrs. Garrett complied. Sergeant Bell contacted Roger, and used a ruse that he needed to speak to Roger concerning a different matter. Roger agreed to go to KPD Headquarters upon his return to Knoxville.

At approximately 5:50pm, Roger arrived at KPD Headquarters. Tony Arias approached him and asked if he was in fact Roger Garrett, and he replied he was. Tony identified himself as "Detective Arias with the El Paso Sheriff's Office" and advised

Roger he was under arrest for the murder of Chester Garrett in 1977. Roger was clearly stunned and visibly paled. Tony advised Roger of his Miranda Rights. After a few seconds, Roger seemed to regain his composure and stated he would invoke his right to counsel.

Tony could tell Roger was trying very hard to appear as if he had not been rattled by the news, but he clearly was. At that moment, thirty-six years of murder and lies just caught up to him.

Tony informed Roger that his mother, Lisbeth Garrett, was also being arrested for Chester Garrett's murder. Roger remained silent. Roger made small talk as they waited for transportation to the Knoxville jail. He asked Tony if this was his first time in Knoxville, Tony replied that it was. Roger recommended restaurants in Knoxville he thought the detectives would like. It seemed a bit surreal.

As Roger was taken away to be booked, he asked Tony for a favor. He asked if Tony could take his car keys to his wife so she could recover their car. Tony agreed, knowing it was a good opportunity to interview his wife. Roger was booked into the Knox County Detention Facility under a "Fugitive from Justice" charge to await extradition to the State of Texas.

The detectives returned to Roger Garrett's apartment on Arbor Trace Drive and again met with Susan Garrett, Roger's third wife. Tony gave her Roger's car keys and informed her Roger was under arrest and charged with murdering his step-father, Chester Garrett. Mrs. Garrett was surprised but remained calm. She said she did not believe her husband was capable of committing murder. She said she had been married to Roger for eighteen years but had known him for twenty. Tony asked if he had ever told her how his father was killed, and she said Roger claimed his father was murdered on duty while investigating "nefarious individuals" in a drug-related case. She added that Roger found out he was adopted the day his father died. Tony also informed Susan Garrett that Roger's mother Lisbeth had also been arrested for the murder. Mrs. Garrett matter-of-factly replied she didn't know Roger's mother very well. At that point the detectives excused themselves and left. Tony couldn't stop thinking if his own wife had just been informed Tony had been arrested for murdering his father, that there would have been a much stronger reaction of disbelief. Tony felt as if he had told her Roger had been arrested for jaywalking.

As they drove away from Garrett's apartment complex, Tony called Jackie Conner to give her the news she had been waiting to hear for the last thirty-six years. It was late in the evening, but he could not wait to give her the good news. Jackie answered and Tony said, "Jackie, this is Tony Arias with the Sheriff's Office, and I am calling to tell you that we just booked Roger Garrett into the Knoxville jail for the murder of your brother, Chester."

Jackie let out a short yell, followed by sobs. She was elated and emotionally overwhelmed. Tony quickly explained to her the developments set in motion after Patrick finally came forward to provide the missing pieces to the puzzle. Jackie thanked Tony for not giving up and continuing with the case throughout the years.

Tony told her it had been an honor to finally bring some closure to her and her family, and to bring justice to an American hero. After that call, Tony allowed himself a little mental break to relish the moment. He thought a bit as they rode in the rental car. Tony looked at his partner and said, "Jorge, I've never had a martini, but this seems like the perfect time to have one."

So they did.

Chapter 56

Minutes after Roger was arrested in Kentucky, EPSO CAP Detectives Louis Santibanez, Jerome Washington and Rafael Chavez arrested Lisbeth in Room 107 at a Super 8 Motel on Gateway East in El Paso. Lisbeth was transported to Sheriff's Office headquarters where she was interviewed by Sergeant Belknap and Detective Irene Anchondo. Lisbeth was advised of her Miranda Rights but agreed to speak with detectives. During the interview, she did not invoke her right to silence but denied having any participation in the murder of her husband, Chester Garrett. Lisbeth was booked into the El Paso County Detention Facility.

The next day a search warrant was executed at Lisbeth's home at 8908 Gallic Court, El Paso. One of the items detectives were looking for was a wooden plaque that may have held a presentation knife. This item was not found. A box containing other wooden plaques was located and photographed. Even after actions taken by Adult Protective Services and Patrick's efforts to clean house, it was still in complete disarray and was clearly the home of a hoarder. Some rooms were impossible to enter without removing large piles of boxes and debris. Detectives were forced to wear protective suits and masks as protection against overall filth.

The detectives, investigators and prosecutors who worked on the case in 1977 were no longer working in those capacities. Some had left to pursue other ventures, some retired and several others, unfortunately, were deceased. Tony Arias followed the same process in locating the detectives as he did in finding witnesses. He sent whatever information he had available to analysts in law enforcement support centers to search for contact information for the original detectives.

Fred Timmons, the lead sergeant for EPSD CAP in 1977, was now retired but lived in El Paso. Detective John Omohundro was now Manager of Security for a petroleum corporation and resided near Houston. Detective Reginald Yearwood lived in Odessa, Texas, retired after finishing his law enforcement career as

Sheriff of Ector County. Detective Jesus "Chuy" Reyes stayed in El Paso after rising to EPSD Chief Deputy. Chuy Reyes left EPSD in the 1980s, and was currently a general manager with the El Paso County Water District.

Tony contacted these former EPSD detectives with copies of their original reports to refresh their memories in preparation as potential trial witnesses. Tony met and interviewed each detective to get his perspective on what had occurred 36 years before. What were they sure of? What were they unsure of? Had anything happened over the years that gave them a different understanding of what happened in 1977?

Tony knew too well that CAP detectives are constantly inundated with high profile cases. Murders, sexual assaults and kidnappings keep coming hard and fast. Detectives often feel they're drowning in an ocean of cases but are loathe to ask for help because the others are in the same predicament. So, CAP detectives simply learn to "handle it" by prioritizing casework by its emergency status at the moment.

Sometimes information is left out of a police report. The investigator might think his partner will cover it in his report, or perhaps at the time they might feel it's not pertinent enough to document. Whatever the reason, undocumented facts can haunt an investigation, even decades later.

All investigators make decisions or take actions they wish they could do over again. Mistakes are made, particularly when a detective is working with partial information, tired, stressed, and with only their gut instinct to guide them. It stings when good faith mistakes are thrown in an investigator's face on the stand during a suppression hearing or during trial, but it is highly educational. You get raked over the coals; you better learn from it.

Chapter 57

On February 23, 2013, less than a week after Lisbeth and Roger were arrested, J.W. Gee, the original lead Army CID investigator, contacted Detective Tony Arias. J.W. Gee immediately said this case had bothered him for the last thirty-five years. J.W. added he had assigned this case to a "cold case squad" he formed of hand-selected Army CID agents, but the investigation was ultimately dropped with a change in army investigative priorities.

In 1977, J.W. Gee worked closely with El Paso Sheriff's Department detectives during their investigation. He assisted with any lead that needed to be handled by Army CID or through army channels. J.W. recalled a conversation with Sheriff's Detective John Omohundro just after the aborted consent search of Lisbeth Garrett's home. J.W. remembered John telling him that John was in the laundry room next to the kitchen and saw what he believed to be blood spatter on the wall. J.W. said John Omohundro brought this to the attention of other detectives, and was overheard by Lisbeth Garrett's attorney, who immediately ordered all law enforcement personnel out of the house. J.W. asked Tony if there was any documentation of this in the reports. Tony, caught off guard, informed J.W. there was nothing in the case file about blood in the laundry room, only the garage.

J.W. said he worked alongside FBI agents following leads involving members of a basketball team coached by MAJ Garrett, but ultimately these leads went nowhere. J.W. told Sergeant Belknap and Detective Arias he always believed MAJ Garrett was killed at the Backus house by Roger Garrett, who hit him in the head with a baseball bat or crowbar, and by Lisbeth Garrett who stabbed him with a knife.

Following the interview with J.W. Gee, Tony Arias called John Omohundro, who confirmed he told J.W. Gee about blood in the house, except it was in the kitchen, not the laundry room. John Omohundro told Tony he was in the kitchen while Lisbeth and her attorney, Mike Cohen, were in a hallway by the kitchen, or possibly an adjacent bedroom. John Omohundro looked under the kitchen table and saw what looked like drops of dried blood or paint runs on the wall behind the table. John Omohundro said he touched it and could feel the contour of dried blood drips. Omohundro tried to discretely call to Sergeant Fred Timmons what he found. Attorney Mike Cohen overheard John Omohundro and came into the kitchen with Lisbeth, verbally revoked the consent to search, and ordered the investigators to leave the house.

Tony Arias was stunned by this revelation. After a moment, he told John Omohundro there was no report in the case file or any documentation of John's discovery of blood on the kitchen wall. It was John Omohundro's turn to be stunned. Tony explained that John himself wrote the Sheriff's Office report about the consent search; it was a short report that listed the officers involved, and noted at 2:10pm, "Officers noticed what appeared to be blood on the south wall of the garage." The next and final entry in the report was at 5:00pm: "Officers completed their search and departed the scene….investigation continues…"

John Omohundro had no explanation as to why the blood in the kitchen or the officers' sudden order to exit was never documented. No doubt a lapse of 36 years affects memory, but both John and Tony agreed it was a damned shame.

Chapter 58

Roger Garrett remained incarcerated at Knoxville County Jail awaiting an Identification and Extradition hearing. Perhaps he was tired of that particular jail, because he signed a waiver to cancel the extradition hearing, which allowed EPSO to transport him to Texas. He was being held on a "Fugitive from Justice" charge in Knoxville, but once he was brought to El Paso, he would formally be charged with murder.

On February 27, 2013, Detective Tony Arias and EPSO deputy Edward Chavira escorted Roger Garrett to El Paso from Knoxville. Usually EPSO deputies from the Warrants and Fugitive Section transport prisoners, but in this case Tony went along in case Roger said anything incriminating on the flight. He had already "lawyered up" so Tony would not speak about anything related to the case, but if Roger made an unsolicited comment that helped their case, it was fair game.

They took custody of Roger at the Knox County Detention Facility. Roger greeted Tony as if they were old friends. Roger asked if Tony had a good flight and was very amenable. On the return flight, during a layover at DFW Airport, Roger commented that he was a member of the football team his senior year at Burges High School, and he could bench press 200 pounds. This statement was not solicited from Roger by either Tony or Deputy Chavira, but was significant in that the District Attorney needed to show a jury that eighteen-year-old Roger Garrett was physically capable of the blow that killed a much larger man like MAJ Garrett, and able to move the heavy body into the back seat of a Volkswagen Beetle. The jury could envision a young and strong Roger Garrett in 1977 instead of the 55 year old man before them in the courtroom.

Upon arrival in El Paso, Garrett was taken before District Judge Mike Herrera, who gave him his Magistrate Warning and signed two search warrants for Buccal Swabs, one for Roger Garrett and the other for Lisbeth Ann Garrett. Both search warrants were executed by Detective Jerome Washington. Roger Garrett was booked into the El Paso County Detention Facility on First Degree

Murder.

A buccal swab is a way of collecting DNA by a large cotton swab dragged along the inside of a person's cheek. These swabs were sent to the DPS lab to develop a DNA profile for Roger and Lisbeth to be compared to items in evidence. Chester Garrett's DNA profile had already been submitted to DPS.

Advances in science and technology to assist investigators in solving crimes have been substantial. Unfortunately, in this case none of the newer sciences played a significant role in bringing the perpetrators to justice. It came down to "old school" police work of tracking down witnesses who provided corroborating information. None of the newer techniques or advancements in science were available in 1977, so it seemed fitting that old school "gumshoe" police work brought in these two offenders who had eluded justice for 36 years.

Chapter 59

When a suspect is in jail awaiting trial, analysis of the inmate's phone calls ("jail calls") becomes extremely important in pursuing investigative leads. The inmate hears a recorded message at the beginning of each call advising their conversation is being monitored and recorded. Since there is no expectation of privacy, any utterance made by the inmate can be used against the inmate at trial. Jail calls are available for a detective to review, with the exception of calls between the inmate and his attorney.

During Roger Garrett's incarceration, Tony Arias reviewed his jail calls daily. During one call, he heard Roger discussing paperwork pertaining to a business called "Hire-A-Liar" that Patrick Garrett filed with the El Paso County Clerk's office in 1985. It was clear Roger's attorneys would use the business name to discredit Patrick Garrett during trial. Tony realized they had to contact Patrick, sort it out and advise the district attorney's office.

On May 17, 2013, Tony and Jerome Washington met with Patrick Garrett regarding "Hire-A-Liar." Patrick said that in 1985 his mother Lisbeth was a regular reader of tabloid magazines, and in one she read an article about a business called "Hire-a-Liar." Patrick explained the premise was he could be hired to provide an alibi for someone in trouble; a cheating spouse or a gambler, for example. Patrick said his mother believed it was a good idea for Patrick to register the name in El Paso County to prevent another person from using that name. Patrick said he never actually opened or operated the business. Regardless, Tony suffered an immediate headache at the thought of his primary witness taking steps to become a professional liar.

Chapter 60

When Detectives Arias and Andrade interviewed Theresa Heffelfinger, Roger's second wife, in January 2013, she said she was introduced to Roger by Debra Drake. On June 16, 2013, Detectives Arias and Washington interviewed Debra Drake.

Debra said she used to hang out with Roger Garrett in 1978 when she was a sophomore at Coronado High School. Debra suspected Roger wanted to date her, but she was not interested. Roger and his fraternity brothers were attending the University of Texas at El Paso (UTEP). She described him as being very athletic; he would do gymnastic moves on the dance floor when they went dancing in Ciudad Juarez, Mexico.

Debra said that about a month after meeting Roger, they walked to a park near Roger's apartment. They sat on a park bench drinking beer when Roger told her his father had been a very important person: a high ranking military man who was involved in important operations. Debra added it sounded to her like Roger's father was doing covert missions for the government, maybe CIA or FBI. Roger became upset and told her his world had turned upside down, and Roger was trying to deal with it. Roger told Debra his mother told him his father was beating her, that she was in fear for her life, and that they had to stop him. Roger said he had to protect his mother, and that's why they had to kill him. Roger told Debra he and his mother devised a plan to surprise his father whereby they would knock him unconscious and kill him.

Roger explained to Debra he and his mother realized they could not overpower his father, so they needed an element of surprise to carry out the murder. Roger said he and his mother first considered shooting his father during his daily jog but abandoned that idea.

Instead, they lured his father to a location where he could be surprised and knocked unconscious. Roger told Debra he hid in a laundry room or washroom and surprised his father from behind by striking him in the back of the head with a heavy wooden object, like a baseball bat or two-by-four. His father was knocked unconscious. Debra remembered that Roger told her they also stabbed his father with a knife. Roger and his mother put his father's body in his car and drove it out into a remote desert area of El Paso. Roger told Debra the killing was very well planned, and while he and his mother were suspects, the police were unable to prove they did it.

Roger also told Debra he didn't know how neighbors didn't catch on because they cleaned the blood out of the garage using chemicals, and the residue ran from the garage to the street.

Debra told the detectives she didn't believe Roger and thought he was only trying to impress her, and for this reason did not report it to police. She left El Paso for approximately a year, and lost contact with Roger until 1991, when she introduced Roger to her good friend Terry Heffelfinger. Roger and Terry dated and later married, but their marriage didn't last long. After their divorce, Terry told Debra that Roger had confessed to her that he and his mother had killed his father. Debra realized then what Roger told her in 1978 about killing his father was true. Terry told Debra she was going to the police about the murder, and Debra asked Terry to contact her when she did.

In fact, Terry was interviewed by Captain Gary Gabbert in 1996. Terry told Captain Gabbert essentially the same facts she later told the detectives, as evidenced by a report discovered in the long-missing case file. Terry did not tell Debra she talked to Gabbert, and she and Debra didn't speak of the murder again, at least not until they were contacted by Detective Arias.

Chapter 61

On July 2, 2013, EPSO Detectives Tony Arias and Louis Santibanez interviewed Elaine Berry, the childhood friend and neighbor of the Garrett family on Backus Street. Elaine Berry said she met Roger Garrett when they both attended Burges High School. They were close friends; she spent a lot of time at the Garrett house. They socialized five to six nights a week playing cards. Elaine first started going to the Garrett house in about 1974, and at that time Roger's parents were still together. She remembered Mr. Garrett playing basketball with Roger and younger brother Patrick. They seemed like an average family at first.

Elaine Berry said after a couple of years passed, Roger claimed Mr. Garrett had beaten him and his mother on several occasions, and they could not forgive him. Roger was a wrestler, and although he was short, he had broad shoulders. He also had a bad temper. Elaine recalled Roger telling her he was going to take Mr. Garrett down with a wrestling move some day. Roger implied he was going to kill his father, he hated him that much. Elaine continued visiting the Garrett house until she left for college. In the time she spent at the Garrett household, she never witnessed Mr. Garrett strike or hit either Roger or Mrs. Garrett.

Elaine Berry recalled Mrs. Garrett and Roger sitting around talking about how to commit the "perfect murder", and they went to movies and read anything having to do with a "perfect murder." This took place a few days prior to Mr. Garrett's murder. When Mrs. Garrett and Roger talked about the "perfect murder", they would send Patrick off to bed or to do his homework.

Elaine Berry said both Roger and Patrick idolized Mrs. Garrett, and whenever she spoke they focused on her. The boys never spoke badly about their mother to Elaine, and they did whatever she told them to do. Once Roger had a girlfriend that Mrs. Garrett didn't like, and he dropped her immediately.

When Elaine Berry was home from college for Thanksgiving 1976, she visited the Garrett house and Mrs. Garrett told her she did not love Mr. Garrett, there was nothing good about him, and if it had been financially possible she would have divorced him. As long as she had known the Garretts, Mrs. Garrett had been strictly opposed to drinking, but now she was drinking heavily. When Elaine came by, Mrs. Garrett would encourage her to join her in drinking a white russian. When Elaine declined, Mrs. Garrett informed her that the drink had milk in it as if this would make a difference. Roger would drink white russians or whatever alcoholic beverage his mother was having.

During the 1976 Christmas holidays, Elaine again came home from college and visited the Garrett residence. She remembered seeing a baseball bat by the back door, leaning against the washer and dryer. She usually went into the Garrett home through the garage and laundry room. She asked Roger about the bat, and he told her if his father ever came near him or his mother again, he would beat his father to death with the bat. The next evening, the bat was not there.

Elaine Berry last saw Mr. Garrett during the 1976 Christmas holiday season at the Garrett residence. Although Mr. and Mrs. Garrett were separated, Mr. Garrett came to do chores around the house. During that last visit, Mr. Garrett seemed remarkably detached and defeated as Mrs. Garrett and Roger viciously teased Mr. Garrett. They swore at him and teased him about some past event unknown to Elaine. Elaine thought it very unusual, as Mr. Garrett did not tolerate cursing, yet he was being cursed at by Roger and Mrs. Garrett without objection. On this occasion Roger told Elaine, "We caught him again," and said he and his mother had caught Mr. Garrett with another woman.

In early January 1977, before she returned to school, Elaine visited the Garrett house one morning, but she didn't remember the date. Mrs. Garrett told Elaine Mr. Garrett was possibly missing as no one had seen him since he had played basketball the day before. Mrs. Garrett said she didn't like the guys he was playing with and wouldn't be surprised if they found Mr. Garrett's body out in the desert. Elaine returned to the Garrett house a few hours later to see if they wanted to play cards that evening. When she arrived, Roger was washing Mrs. Garrett's large white car while Mrs. Garrett stood by. Elaine thought this strange as she had never seen Roger wash her car before. She also noticed the car had new tires and remarked about them. Mrs. Garrett told her they were going to Disneyland.

Later that day, Roger showed Elaine some Polaroid photographs. One photo showed the Garrett's backyard grass being burned. Another photo was of a trash barrel in the Garrett backyard and fire coming out of the barrel while Roger, Mrs. Garrett and a third person were throwing items into the barrel. Elaine could tell they were drinking because they were holding cups. The third photo was of Mrs. Garrett, Roger, and a third person smiling and dancing like it was a celebration. Elaine could not tell if the third person in the photographs was Patrick. Roger mentioned they had a party the night before, and Elaine wondered why she had not been invited.

When Elaine returned to college, her father informed her of Mr. Garrett's death. This prompted her to write the letter to the Sheriff's Department in January 1977, where it remained in the case file all those years.

Chapter 62

On August 27, 2013, Tony contacted Katherine Devaney, Roger Garrett's first wife. Katherine said she and Roger were married in 1982, and divorced in 1989. Katherine was aware Roger had been arrested for murder, having been informed of his arrest by her and Roger's daughter, Sabrina Lopez. Katherine said she knew Roger's father was dead but did not know he had been murdered. She said she did not get along with Roger's mother, Lisbeth Garrett, and described her as a "strange woman." Lisbeth told Katherine she was going to have a deformed child because Roger used a lot of drugs. Katherine said that was true; Roger did use cocaine, marijuana and LSD. Katherine said they lived at Lisbeth's house on Gallic Court for a short time, and while Lisbeth wanted nothing to do with her granddaughter Sabrina, when her lady friends were over she would "love" on Sabrina and hug her.

Katherine told Tony Arias that Roger's drug use played a big part in their divorce and said Roger spent time in prison for drugs while they were married. After they split, Roger wanted Katherine to return and live with his mother, but Katherine wanted nothing more to do with Roger or Lisbeth. Katherine said she filed for divorce, and she and Sabrina moved onto the Navajo Reservation. Roger and his mother tried to kidnap Sabrina from her on the reservation, but Navajo Tribal Police stopped Roger and Lisbeth in the vehicle Lisbeth was driving and rescued Sabrina. Roger and Lisbeth were arrested and ultimately banned from the reservation. Theresa said Patrick also kidnapped his children from his ex-wife, and Ms. Heffelfinger believes Lisbeth was behind that crime as well. Katherine said Lisbeth often tried to frighten her and described Lisbeth as "domineering, very odd and weird." She said the last time she spoke to Roger was when their daughter was 18 years of age.

On August 20, 2013, Tony contacted Robert Sherwin. Mr. Sherwin was an army Lieutenant at Fort Bliss in 1977 and was the basketball team coach along with MAJ Garrett. 1LT Sherwin was initially interviewed by EPSD the day Garrett's body was found.

1LT Sherwin said that he met and spoke with MAJ Garrett the evening before about his pending assignment to Italy. Mr. Sherwin asked MAJ Garrett if he was taking his family to Italy, and Major Garrett said he was separated from his wife and was not going to take his family to Italy.

Tony provided Mr. Sherwin a copy of his 1977 statement. After reviewing the statement, Mr. Sherwin said he recalled his interview and the contents of the statement, but because of the time lapse since 1977 he did not recall anything more. Tony felt Mr. Sherwin's conversation with MAJ Garrett was vital as it refuted Lisbeth's and Roger Garrett's declarations that they were going to Italy as a family unit with MAJ Garrett.

Chapter 63

Roger Garrett's trial was scheduled to begin with jury selection on Monday, October 14, 2013. As the date loomed, the District Attorney's Office offered Roger a deal of 10 years' probation if he would testify against his mother Lisbeth Garrett. Roger rejected the offer.

On Wednesday, October 16, 2013, Roger Garrett's jury trial opened before the Honorable Judge Marcos Lizarraga in 168th District Court, in El Paso, Texas. The prosecutors were Assistant District Attorneys Denise Butterworth and Kyle Myers. Roger's defense attorneys were Matthew Dekoatz and Ruben Morales.

Detective Tony Arias suffered an ironic status that plagues investigators at trial. He had spent the previous seven years on the Garrett investigation and knew it better than anyone. He was the reference book of all things Chester Garrett for the Prosecution. He was not scheduled to be a witness, but because he could potentially be required to testify on any given part of the investigation, he was not allowed to witness any of the trial he had worked so hard to bring about. Tony was relegated to killing time outside the courtroom doors and found it frustratingly tedious.

A personal issue also bothered Tony. Because of the trial, he had to miss his son's graduation from Army Ranger School in Fort Benning, Georgia. How ironic that Tony would miss his son being awarded his "Ranger Tab" because of the trial of a murdered Ranger's son.

ADA Kyle Myers made the State's opening statement. He described how Chester Garrett was found in the desert and how his family repeatedly avoided cooperation with police. He described evidence discovered at the Backus house and how consent-to-search was revoked when Detective Omohundro saw what he thought was blood in the kitchen. He described the state of MAJ Garrett's BOQ room after the murder; lights on, half eaten sandwich and open can of Mountain Dew. ADA Myers described how Roger confessed his involvement in the murder to Debra Drake in 1978. He described

Patrick Garrett's recollections of the strange events occurring in his home after coming home from the movies that night, and how Patrick confronted Roger years later in the presence of Patrick's wife, Jeanne Patterson. ADA Myers talked about how law enforcement approached Patrick three separate times before he cooperated in 2013, and his reasons for doing so. During Myer's Opening Statement, defense counsel objected several times resulting in multiple conferences between the judge and attorneys. It was going to be a contentious trial.

Attorney Matthew Dekoatz gave the Defense's opening statement. Dekoatz noted how Debra Drake introduced Roger to his second wife, Theresa Heffelfinger, while Debra and Theresa were best friends. How could Debra allow her best friend to marry a confessed killer? He stated Roger loved his father, even though his father was a professional killer, a violent man who died a violent death. Mr. Dekoatz described Patrick as emotionally and mentally confused his entire life, and now a dangerous, unstable con man. He advised the jury to watch Patrick closely and remember he was a "flip-flop, flim-flam" person not worthy of belief. He also told the jury that the other people who Roger made admissions to all knew each other, and Roger's statements marinated and simmered among them for 37 years. Dekoatz closed his statement with a reminder that no physical evidence -- DNA, fingerprints or a murder weapon -- existed.

The prosecution's first witness was Debra Drake, who recounted her relationship, friends only, with Roger when she was in high school and how she introduced him to Theresa Heffelfinger in 1990. She described Roger's 1978 graphic confession of how he and his mother had killed his father.

ADA Butterworth passed the witness to the defense, and Mr. Dekoatz did his best to discredit Debra's testimony. Debra testified she didn't believe Roger's confession in 1978 because she thought Roger was simply trying to impress her, nor did she tell Theresa about his confession for the same reason.

The prosecution's second witness was Theresa Heffelfinger, who testified Debra introduced her to Roger; that they married a few months later, but were only married for about 15 months. About four months into the marriage they were already having problems, and during an argument Roger told her he and his mother killed his father. Roger told Theresa he ambushed his father with a baseball bat in their home. His mother stabbed his father as well, then they dumped the body in the desert. They proceeded to get rid of their clothes, the bat, the knife and changed the tires on his mother's car.

Defense attorney Ruben Morales cross-examined the witness and stressed Theresa' poor relationship with Roger during their marriage and insinuated that Theresa was just making assumptions about what Roger told her.

The prosecution called its next witness, Patrick Garrett.

Tony Arias knew Patrick was both the prosecution's best and worse witness. The EPSO CAP team had done as much as possible to help his credibility by corroborating details he provided, yet his veracity was like a slice of Swiss cheese, full of holes. Patrick's mental processes were such that he had difficulty describing a truthful series of events the same way twice. Prosecutors Butterworth and Myers knew they were in for a fight. They were two of the District Attorney's Office's top prosecutors, and they knew the defense's main strategy was to impeach Patrick as a witness.

Just as justice had caught up to Roger and Lisbeth, the after-effects of Patrick's life choices were also catching up to him, to the detriment of the case against Roger.

Throughout the trial, this roller coaster pattern of highs and lows persisted. One day things indicated a guilty verdict was just around the corner, and the next they looked bleak for the prosecution, as if they'd be lucky to get a "hung jury."

On the stand Patrick gave his story and revealed why it took so long to report that Roger had admitted he and Lisbeth had murdered his father. The subject of the business "Hire-a- Liar" was brought up and Patrick admitted he had in fact registered the name.

Patrick recounted events from January 3, 1977; he and a neighbor friend went to the movies on a school night, his mom was supposed to pick him up but didn't, his house was dark and no one was home when he returned to his neighbor's house, after a while he saw his porch light on, Roger let him in and "corralled" him to bed without supper, the next morning Roger brought him a bowl of cereal in his room, and sent him to school without going into the kitchen. Patrick testified Roger drove him home from school and told him his father was killed in an accident. He said the following Saturday Roger made Patrick help him clean the garage floor with

Muriatic Acid to clean a large red evaporated stain. Patrick said when they hosed the mess into the driveway it stained the drive and street gutter white.

Patrick testified that in 1990, after he married Jeanne Brock, they stayed with his mother at 8908 Gallic Court in El Paso. In December 1990, Roger came home to visit and confessed to Patrick he and their mother killed Chester Garrett. Roger gave details of the murder to Patrick. Patrick was shocked, and told his wife about Roger's confession, but couldn't bring himself to go to police. Patrick testified he was approached by police in 1995 and in 2006, but refused to cooperate until 2013. Patrick stated his change of heart was due to becoming a Christian after his 16 year old son Ian died. Patrick said he approached Roger in 2010, after he converted, and tried to convince Roger to go to the police and confess to save his soul.

Matthew Dekoatz cross-examined Patrick. He opened by asking Patrick about his email address. When Patrick confirmed his email address, Mr. Dekoatz produced an embarrassing email message Patrick denied was his. Dekoatz lectured Patrick on telling the truth and insinuated Patrick was a liar, under-employed, had a criminal record and learning disabilities.

Prosecution's next witness was Jeanne Patterson, who testified she was married to Patrick Garrett for five years and had two children with him. She testified that in December 1990, Roger visited them at Lisbeth Garrett's house on Gallic Court. During this visit Patrick and Roger had a serious discussion about Chester Garrett's murder. Lisbeth came into the room and argued with the boys when she heard the topic. Jeanne testified she heard Lisbeth say, "I guess I raised a bunch of idiots", to which Roger retorted, "No, you've raised a bunch of killers." Roger and Patrick went outside to continue their conversation while Jeanne went to a bathroom to avoid any further confrontation with Lisbeth. The bathroom window opened into the garage, and Jeanne saw Lisbeth "hovering" in the dark garage trying to overhear the boys' conversation through the garage door. Jeanne went to bed, and later when Patrick came in he told Jeanne that Roger confessed the murder to Patrick while they were outside.

Matthew Dekoatz cross-examined Jeanne Patterson with a couple of soft questions about dates of moving and dismissed the witness.

The next witness was former El Paso County Sheriff's Department Detective Jesus Reyes, who testified he was one of the detectives on site when MAJ Garrett's body was found, and was at Garrett's BOQ room. Detective Reyes testified to conditions of both scenes and evidence recovered at both. He described the unwillingness of Garrett family members to cooperate with the investigation and the conditions at the Backus house, particularly the stained driveway.

Mr. Dekoatz cross-examined him about the relationship between the El Paso County Sheriff's Department and the Army Criminal Investigation Division, and noted that both agencies had different suspects. Detective Reyes also testified that no physical evidence tied Roger to the desert crime scene.

The Prosecution's next witness was Christine Ceniceros, a Texas DPS Forensic Scientist who specialized in DNA testing. Ms. Ceniceros testified DNA testing was not available in 1977, and that she recently tested the sheetrock sample removed from the Backus garage and determined there was human blood, but was unable to retrieve any DNA identification. Defense attorney Dekoatz interrupted with a request for a Voir Dire Examination (out of hearing of the jury) of DPS laboratory test standards and successfully had Ms. Ceniceros' statements voided to the jury.

The next witness was retired LTC Harrell Hall, MAJ Garrett's commander in Fort Bliss. LTC Hall testified he gave notification of MAJ Garrett's death to Lisbeth Garrett, and recounted how Lisbeth and the oldest son were both wearing matching terrycloth robes in the afternoon, which he thought strange. LTC Hall described MAJ Garrett as a highly decorated soldier and a great executive officer who cared about his soldiers.

Matthew Dekoatz cross-examined by asking if LTC Hall told Roger he was adopted while they were at MAJ Garrett's funeral. LTC Hall stated he did not.

The next witness was Juan Contin, MD, Chief Medical Examiner for El Paso County, who testified about MAJ Garrett's wounds, and stated cause of death was a combination of the blows to the head and the stab wounds; the blows to the head incapacitated him and would have killed him over time, but the stab wounds probably caused Garrett to bleed to death first. Mr. Dekoatz' cross-examination was minimal.

The first day of trial was over. Court was adjourned. Tony Arias felt drained as he was briefed by the Assistant DA's. He was feeling slightly off-balance from the games played at trial. Overall, the day seemed to favor the prosecution. The following day would prove to be the part of the roller-coaster ride where one suddenly drops 100 feet going 70 miles per hour.

The trial reconvened next morning. After 45 minutes of intense discussion between the judge, prosecution and defense over witnesses and evidence, the defense called its first witness, Patrick Garrett.

Matthew Dekoatz showed Patrick the same email from the day before, and asked Patrick again if he wrote the email. Patrick again denied being the author of the email. Mr. Dekoatz read the following passages from the email with Patrick's email address:

> "This past Sunday, the 7th, a friend and I were riding two ATVs in a place called the Underground. It is a public and private storage facility in Carthage, Missouri.
>
> "We were approximately 30 feet away now and what we saw were two creatures. One was very tall, at least seven feet, maybe more, and very powerfully built, reddish in color; and the other was smaller, about six feet, but it was not red in color but pale like an albino, and it looked like reptiles. Living, walking, intelligent beings. Not human. Not warm blooded. Reptiles. I know it sounds crazy, but it is true.
>
> "Well, that is my story. I have never had anything strange happen in my life and I am very concerned about this. I can tell you this; I had an urge to kill the things that I saw down there. I don't know if that is a natural reaction as most people.
>
> "And I wish I could do something, anything, to combat or help against these things. Your new friend and partner, Pat Garrett."

Matthew Dekoatz verified the email address again, and Pat Garrett confirmed he lived in Carthage, Missouri at that time. Patrick stated he knew of the storage facility referenced in the email.

Dekoatz read another one:

> "I am a new member and I would like some help. I was in a cave in a place called the Underground. It is in Carthage, Missouri. It's an underground storage facility for commercial government contracts. We saw a reptilian creature man thing. I called the sheriffs as soon as my cell phone cleared the cave. Thank you for your time. Pat Garrett."

Pat Garrett testified he did not write those email passages. He claimed his email account was somehow "hacked."

Dekoatz turned the witness over to the prosecution for cross-examination, and the prosecution declined. Patrick was dismissed, after which Dekoatz made a motion to impeach Patrick as a witness because of lack of candor. The judge overruled Dekoatz' wishes but gave him another opportunity to examine Patrick.

Patrick was called back to the stand. Dekoatz asked him if he ever shared the reptilian people stories with family members, such as his cousin Christine Myerson. Patrick testified he had shown Christine the same email messages as an example of his email account being hacked, not in the sense that he believed in reptile people. Dekoatz became disgusted and passed the witness.

ADA Kyle Meyers asked Patrick a few questions about the paranormal website he visited, how someone could have gotten his email address, and dismissed the witness.

The defense's next witness was DPS Forensic Scientist Christine Ceniceros. Matthew Dekoatz reviewed how DNA evidence was gathered and processed. Ms. Ceniceros testified none of the DNA collected from the Volkswagen matched Roger's DNA profile, and Dekoatz passed the witness for cross-examination.

ADA Denise Butterworth made a quick cross by verifying none of Chester Garrett's DNA was discovered in evidence taken 38 years before, and that obviously Chester Garrett was the regular driver of the vehicle.

The defense next called Robert Snelson, Roger's high school friend and neighbor, who Roger visited on the night of the murder. Robert testified Roger came to his house late that night, to help Robert with an English paper for school. Robert stated the written statements he gave previously to police were accurate, but after more than 30 years he had no personal recollection of details. The defense had Robert Snelson read his prior statements to the jury. On cross-examination The prosecution went over details presented in the statements.

The jury was released for lunch. Matthew Dekoatz immediately requested a Voir Dire Examination, for the Judge's benefit only, of a witness who had information regarding Patrick's testimony about reptilian humans. The judge agreed.

The next witness was Christine Myerson, daughter of Susan Garrett, Roger's third wife. Dekoatz asked her to tell the Judge whatever Patrick had told her about "lizard people." Christine testified that in 2010, Patrick visited them in El Paso, and Patrick told her he believed in reptilian shape-shifters. Patrick believed the President of the United States was a shape-shifter, and that Patrick had had a personal encounter with them. Christine said Patrick told her when he lived in Missouri he entered a large underground storage facility with a friend, and multiple 12 foot tall reptile statues came to life and chased them out of the cave.

The attorneys and judge had a conference, and Dekoatz requested a ruling from the Judge on whether the court would accept Ms. Myerson's testimony. The request was complicated by the fact that Ms. Myerson was not expected to be a witness, and had been in the courtroom to hear other witnesses testify, which is usually not allowed. The Judge noted the complexity of the defense's request as a question of whether Patrick could be impeached as a witness because he was not stable or because he lied in front of the jurors. Either possibility raised other legal and ethical issues. The Judge stated his decision to personally listen to a recording of Patrick's statement to the police to decide if Patrick was lucid and credible. The judge gave the defense an option to allow Ms. Myerson to be examined before the jury but in exchange the prosecution would be allowed to play the entire two-hour recording of Patrick's statement for the jury as well. Dekoatz withdrew his request.

The jury was reseated and Dekoatz called his next witness, Patrick Garrett. Dekoatz immediately questioned Patrick about his connection to the business "Hire-A-Liar". Patrick explained he hadn't actually opened the business; he only registered the name. Dekoatz read Patrick the emails regarding the reptilian creatures, and

Patrick again denied writing them and denied telling Christine Myerson he had seen the creatures.

Patrick was dismissed, and Dekoatz once again asked the Judge if he could put Christine Myerson on the stand. The Judge agreed, provided that Dekoatz limit his questions specifically to Patrick's impeachment as a witness.

The next witness was Christine Myerson. She repeated her testimony about Patrick's belief in reptilian shape-shifters and that the President of the United States was a reptile creature. Dekoatz passed the witness to the prosecution, who simply verified that Christine loved her step-father Roger and wanted to help him any way she could.

The next witness was Roger Garrett.

Dekoatz opened by asking Roger to describe his father, Chester Garrett. Roger stated:

> "My father was the highest decorated officer to come out of Vietnam. He was 35 years old when he was murdered. He was a bigger-than-life man that invoked passion in people. He took care of young soldiers, young people. He mentored. He guided.
>
> "He was a professional athlete who was born on Saint Thomas in the Virgin Islands, one of ten kids. He used to wash cars to make extra money because he was a hustler. He signed a contract, minor league, with the Chicago Cubs and pitched with them in Mesa, Arizona, until he tore a rotator cuff.
>
> "He was 18 years old when he decided to join the army. Well, it was the best thing that could have happened to our country. He got his GED. Worked his way up through the enlisted ranks. Got his college degree at North Carolina State and the University of Nebraska with a Master's in business. He became a commissioned officer, major, in the field at the age of 26. He was on the list from Leavenworth to go to General school.
>
> "He was given the best reviews of any officer that I've ever seen anywhere. And people who are in the know called him a soldier's soldier and a man of men.

One of the best combat operatives the Vietnam stage ever had. He went to Vietnam three times. He volunteered all three times. He was a Green Beret."

Actually, Roger misspoke on several points in his description of his father. Chester Garrett was one of the highest decorated soldiers to come out of Vietnam, but he was not the highest. According to the U.S. Army Center for Military History, 245 Medals of Honor, the highest medal for valor possible, were awarded for the Vietnam War. Chester was not one of them. Also, Chester graduated from high school. He did not "get his GED." And Chester did not receive a Master's Degree in business, but he had a Bachelor's Degree.

Dekoatz led Roger through a litany of testimony that stressed Roger's and Chester's close relationship, and what a great father and role model Chester was for Roger. Roger denied he killed his father, and denied telling anyone he killed his father. Roger testified his family's opinion of Patrick was he was a con man, a liar, and not a truthful person. Roger provided an alibi for his actions on the night of the murder similar to statements he gave police in 1977. Roger stated he and Patrick were ordered by their mother to clean the garage floor of transmission fluid and oil. Roger described the extreme use of Muriatic Acid as a cleaning procedure routinely used on post to maintain the military's high standards of cleanliness requirements for dependent housing. Dekoatz passed the witness to ADA Myers.

ADA Kyle Myers and Roger went through his alibi for the night of January 3, 1977, and Myers determined a gap from 7:10pm until 10:30pm that Roger could not account for by witnesses or evidence. Myers badgered Roger about when Patrick spoke truthfully and when he didn't, and about why his ex-wife and his former high school friend would both make up stories about Roger. Roger also admitted he had never contacted the Sheriff's Department to inquire about the status of his father's investigation.

Day Two of the trial concluded.

During the trial Detective Arias listened to recordings of Roger's outgoing jail calls. During one exchange with his wife Susan, Roger was ebullient and expressed certainty he would be found innocent. Susan told Roger she had a bottle of champagne chilled at home to celebrate his release. *Not if I can help it,* thought Tony.

On Monday, October 21, trial reconvened. The judge instructed the jury on elements of murder in the State of Texas, and how to reach a verdict. ADA Kyle Myers and Matthew Dekoatz gave their opposing closing statements to the jury. ADA Myers stated the prosecution knew the murder occurred between 7:30pm and 10:30pm, when neither Roger nor Lisbeth Garrett had an alibi, and advised the jury that Roger and Lisbeth worked together, murdered together, and cleaned up together. Dekoatz offered a theory that Chester was kidnapped from his BOQ on base and killed by persons unknown. Ruben Morales, for the defense, and ADA Denise Butterworth gave their closing statements as well. ADA Butterworth used Roger's 1977 Grand Jury testimony to point out inconsistencies with new information presented in the trial. All four attorneys were intelligent, articulate and passionate.

At 12:17pm the jury was sent away from the courtroom to deliberate Roger's innocence or guilt. At 7:50pm they returned with a verdict. Detective Arias and Sergeant Belknap were finally admitted to the courtroom with a crowd of onlookers. Tony Arias sat next to James Belknap and waited. He prepared himself for the worst. The old adage, "Hope for the best, but prepare for the worst" went through his head. The entire courtroom was tense with anticipation.

The jury foreperson gave the verdict sheet to the bailiff, who passed it to the Judge. The Judge passed it to the Court Clerk and asked him to read page 6. The Clerk read the following:

> "The State of Texas versus Roger Garrett, 20130D01613. Verdict of the Jury: We, the jury, find the defendant, Roger Garrett, guilty of murder as charged in the indictment. "

Tony turned to Sergeant Belknap and asked him if he had heard right. "Guilty?"

Jim Belknap exclaimed, "Yes!"

They jumped up, shook hands and embraced as if they had just won a marathon race, which of course they had, a seven year marathon. Tony quickly looked towards MAJ Garrett's family members. He wanted to soak in their happiness and relief that this first trial was finally over. *One down, one to go*, he thought.

Tony looked over to Roger, who maintained his composure but was obviously stunned. Here was a man who, according to his jail calls, planned to move to Florida and buy a beachfront home with proceeds of a book he planned to pen of how he had been wrongfully charged with murder and beat the rap. He clearly believed he would walk away free.

Roger was not going to have any of that chilled champagne.

Tony went to each of MAJ Garrett's three sisters and hugged them. After all they had gone through together, he felt like part of their family.

The next day, October 22, 2013, the punishment phase commenced. Roger's attorneys asked the District Attorney's Office if Roger could now take the plea deal of 10 years' probation offered him prior to his trial. Roger was now willing to testify against his mother. The DA's Office found Roger's request humorous. After only two hours, the jury handed Roger Garrett a sentence of 40 years imprisonment and a fine of $5,000.

Chapter 64

Two years later, on Thursday, October 15, 2015, Lisbeth Garrett's murder trial opened in 168th District Court before the Honorable Judge Marcos Lizarraga.

This day had been a long time coming. Lisbeth's counsel had filed numerous requests for "continuances"; the Judge complied twice, each time delaying the trial for months at a time. Tony Arias had learned from Roger's intercepted jail calls that Lisbeth was forced to remortgage her house on Gallic Court for more than $100,000 to pay her and Roger's attorneys' fees and to post bond for Lisbeth to get out of jail after her arrest. Lisbeth was unable to make payments on the mortgage debt, and eventually lost the house to foreclosure; she was living in cheap hotels when she was arrested.

Another irony: Presumably Lisbeth used Chester's life insurance money to move the family from Backus Street into the Gallic Court house a few months after killing Chester. If so, Chester's "blood money" went full circle, used first to purchase equity in a home, and then converted to cash to pay legal fees for the persons suspected of killing Chester in the first place. Profits earned from the murder were largely depleted to defend the murderers.

Attorneys Richard Esper and Robert Ramos, both with scrappy junkyard-dog reputations, defended Lisbeth. The prosecutors, ADAs Denise Butterworth and James Montoya, felt confidant after success in prosecuting Roger two years before, but they knew this was no slam-dunk exercise. The prosecution and defense both knew intimately the strong and weak points of the case. Nevertheless, the trial seemed to unfold in a litany of witnesses that benefited the prosecution.

An El Paso Times article on October 17 stated, "friends, neighbors and law enforcement officers all took the stand..." Medical Examiner Juan Contin and retired Lieutenant Colonel Glenn Hall testified to the same facts they had at Roger's trial, as did Patrick Garrett. When he described cleaning the garage floor, Patrick also testified there was a "giant red Kool-Aid stain" like he had never seen that covered most of one side of the garage floor.

The prosecution rested its case on Monday, October 19, and the defense rested the following day without calling any witnesses. The jury heard closing arguments from both sides, during which ADA Butterworth read one of Chester's many spectacular military citations. The jury was riveted. They went into deliberation with a collection of Chester Garrett's citations for valor.

On Wednesday the 21st, the courtroom was silent as the jury's verdict was read. Lisbeth Garrett was found guilty.

Chester's sister Jackie Conner watched as Lisbeth was led out of the courtroom. Jackie heard Patrick call loudly, "Mom…Mom!" Lisbeth ignored him. She didn't break her stride or even attempt to look back at her youngest son.

The next day she was sentenced to 45 years in prison, 5 more years than her son, Roger.

According to the Texas Department of Corrections, Roger Garrett's projected release date from prison is November 11, 2028, when Roger is 70 years old. Lisbeth Garrett's projected release date is November 19, 2033, just before her 95th birthday.

Chapter 65

Reynaldo Cervantes was a senior intelligence manager for a federal law enforcement agency in El Paso, Texas. Rey had no professional ties to the Chester Garrett murder investigation but nevertheless became involved due to his passion for military history. Rey liked to scour estate sales in search of military memorabilia, which he exhaustively researched to compile historical memorials to veterans associated with the memorabilia.

On March 2, 2014, Rey visited an estate sale at 8909 Gallic Court, where the organizer of the sale showed Rey a gym bag of cased medals, documents and photos. Rey immediately recognized a Distinguished Service Cross, the nation's second highest military award for valor. He knew this collection was going to be unique and successfully negotiated its purchase.

Simultaneously, Rey learned from the new home owner, Aldo Reyes, that the previous owner and tenant was Lisbeth Garrett, the wife of the veteran. Aldo told Rey that Mrs. Garrett lost the house to foreclosure after mortgaging it the previous year to raise bail after she was arrested for murdering her veteran husband, Chester Garrett.

Aldo Reyes showed Rey a foot locker full of items belonging to Chester Garrett. Rey found more documents, uniforms, plaques, baseballs, a baseball glove and some Vietnam War souvenirs. He purchased the foot locker as well.

Rey researched the items and Chester Garrett's military career over the next few months. The more Rey studied, the more impressed he became, compelling him to research Chester Garrett's life even more intensively. As he learned of Lisbeth's upcoming trial, Rey contacted Tony Arias, and provided copies and photos of Chester Garrett's citations and medals; the same citations presented to the jury at Lisbeth's trial. Certainly Rey's exhaustive research had an impact on Lisbeth's sentence.

Rey learned that the Special Forces Association, El Paso, Texas Isaac Camacho Chapter IX, had petitioned the Army to commemorate MAJ Garrett by naming a building after him. Rey provided several photographs from his collection to the Isaac Camacho Chapter, which were made into a collage of MAJ Garrett's accomplishments and used at the dedication ceremony of the MAJ Chester Garrett Dining Facility on MacGregor Range, New Mexico in June 2014.

A visit to MAJ Garrett's grave site located at Fort Bliss National Cemetery revealed that Garrett's headstone was plain. The headstone only listed Garret's full name, date of birth, date of death and "Vietnam."

What happened to the military awards? Rey provided copies of Garrett's military award citations to the director of the national cemetery in the hopes of getting a new headstone placed at the gravesite. In May 2015, the Fort Bliss National Cemetery Director contacted Rey and advised a new headstone had arrived, and invited Rey to attend the placement. Rey contacted the Special Forces Association, El Paso, Texas Isaac Camacho Chapter IX and arranged a ceremony that took place just before Memorial Day.

In 2016, Rey forwarded a package of MAJ Garrett's award citations, military orders and other pertinent documents to Steve Franzoni of the El Paso, Texas Isaac Camacho Chapter IX of the Special Forces Association. The package, along with a cover letter from the Special Forces Association, was sent to the U.S. Army Special Forces Regiment, Honors, Awards and Affiliation Program that recognizes those who contributed to the welfare of Civil Affairs, Special Forces and Psychological Operations Regiments. In October 2016, MAJ Chester Garrett was inducted into the Special Forces Regiment's memorial ranks.

Rest in Peace, Chester Garrett

Notes

Chapter 1
El Paso County Sheriff's Department Investigative Report; January 4, 1977
El Paso County Sheriff's Department Crime Scene Photographs; January 4, 1977
El Paso County Sheriff's Department Witness Statement; January 1977
El Paso County Sheriff's Department Office Crime Scene Sketches; January 1977

Chapter 2
Headquarters U.S. Army Vietnam, Distinguish Service Cross citation; General Orders # 5961; November 18, 1967
Interview with John Killingstad; December 17, 2017

Chapter 3
Interview with Jackie Conner, Cheryl Ellington, Gretchen (Gigi) Smith; July 11, 2017
Chester Garrett Baseball Reference; < https://www.baseball-reference.com/register/player.fcgi?id=garret001>

Chapter 4
El Paso County Sheriff's Department Investigative Report; January 4, 1977
U.S. Army Investigative Report; January 4, 1977
El Paso County Sheriff's Department Warnings by Magistrate (Howard Jackson); January 4, 1977
El Paso County Sheriff's Department Affidavit (Robert Sherwin); January 4, 1977
El Paso County Sheriff's Department Affidavit (Harrell Hall); January 4, 1977

Chapter 5
Documentation from the private collection of Reynaldo Cervantes Jr.

Chapter 6
El Paso County Sheriff's Department Evidence Inventory Checklist; January 5, 1977
El Paso County Sheriff's Department Investigative Report; January 5, 1977
Medical Examiner's Autopsy; January 5, 1977
El Paso County Sheriff's Department Warnings by Magistrate (Jennifer Molina); January 5, 1977
County of El Paso, Consent to Search (Eugene Thomas); January 5, 1977

Chapter 7
Obituary of Francis J. Kelly; dated January 4, 1998;
<http://www.nytimes.com/1998/01/04/us/fj-kelly-green-beret-leader-in-vietnam-war-is-dead-at-78.html>

The sixties project;
http://www2.iath.virginia.edu/sixties/HTML_docs/Map.html
Documentation from the private collection of Reynaldo Cervantes Jr.
Hicks, George Sp5; The Observer; date unknown; pg. 3
Kelly, Francis J.; Vietnam Studies U.S. Army Special Forces 1961 – 1971; 1973; pg. 35

Chapter 8
El Paso County Sheriff's Department Warnings by Magistrate (Jennifer Molina); January 6, 1977
County of El Paso, Consent to Search (Jennifer Molina); January 6, 1977
El Paso County Sheriff's Department Warnings by Magistrate (Charles Hicks); January 6, 1977

Chapter 9
El Paso County Sheriff's Department Investigative Report; January 7, 1977
El Paso County Sheriff's Department Affidavit (Joseph Rozman); January 7, 1977
El Paso County Sheriff's Department Affidavit (Erlinda Juarez); January 7, 1977
El Paso Police Department Complaint Report; July 14, 1976
El Paso Police Department Complaint Report; August 3, 1975
Federal Law Enforcement Agency Correspondence; January 7, 1977
John Doussard; El Paso Times; They Gathered For Goodbyes to "The Chief"; January 8, 1977
Chester Garrett's eulogy provided by Harrell Hall

Chapter 10
Headquarters U.S. Army Vietnam; Bronze Star for Valor Citation; General Order # 1763; April 17, 1967

Chapter 11
Federal Law Enforcement Agency Correspondence; January 10, 1977
El Paso County Sheriff's Department Investigative Report; January 8, 1977
El Paso County Sheriff's Department Affidavit (Sharon Turner); January 8, 1977
El Paso County Sheriff's Department Affidavit (Sharon Turner); January 12, 1977
El Paso County Sheriff's Department Investigative Report; January 11, 1977
El Paso County Sheriff's Department Affidavit (Jerrie Pletcher); January 8, 1977
U.S. Army Investigative Report; January 19, 1977

Chapter 12
Headquarters U.S. Army Vietnam; Silver Star Citation; General Order # 733; February 20, 1967

Witness Statement from Sp/4 Marion C. Cartlidge; December 1966

Chapter 13
Grand Jury Transcripts; El Paso County District Clerks Office; January 13, 1977

Chapter 14
HQ's U.S. Army Vietnam; Soldier's Medal; General Orders # 1515; April 5, 1967
Interview with John Killingstad; December 17, 2017

Chapter 15
El Paso County Consent to Search (Lizbeth Ann Garrett); January 13, 1977
El Paso County Sheriff's Department Statement of Facts; January 1977
El Paso County Sheriff's Department Evidence Inventory Check List; January 13, 1977
El Paso County Sheriff's Department Investigative Report; January 13, 1977
El Paso County Sheriff's Department Warnings by Magistrate (Roger Garrett); January 13, 1977
El Paso County Sheriff's Department Warnings by Magistrate (Lizbeth Ann Garrett); January 13, 1977
Multiple interviews with Detectives John Omohundro and Jesus Reyes, Sergeant Fred Timmons and Assistant District Attorney John Cowan in 2018; Reference Garret Murder Investigation

Chapter 16
HQ's U.S. Army Vietnam; Army Commendation Medal for Heroism; General Orders # 2576; June 2, 1967
Military Correspondence from Commander 5th Special Forces Group; Subject: Congratulatory Message; January 1967

Chapter 17
Statement from Elaine Berry; January 11, 1977
Federal Law Enforcement Agency Investigative Report; July 11, 1977
El Paso County Sheriff's Department Investigative Report; January 14, 1977
El Paso County Sheriff's Department Affidavit (Robert Otis Snelson); January 18, 1977
El Paso County Sheriff's Department Affidavit (Harry R. Snelson); January 18, 1977
El Paso County Sheriff's Department Correspondence to Director Federal Bureau of Investigation/FBI Laboratory; Reference Chester Garrett Murder Investigation; January 20, 1977

Federal Bureau of Investigation Correspondence to Mr. Mike Sullivan Jr., Sheriff of El Paso County and Captain Mac D. Stout; Criminal Investigation Division; March 16, 1977
Veterans Administration Correspondence to the El Paso Chief of Police; Reference VA Claim by Lizbeth Garrett; April 13, 1977
Veterans Administration Correspondence to the El Paso Chief of Police; Reference Chester Garrett; May 2, 1977
El Paso County Sheriff's Department Correspondence to the Veterans Administration; Reference Chester Garrett; May 6, 1977
Veterans Administration Correspondence to the El Paso County Sheriff's Department; Reference Chester Garrett; May 19, 1977
Correspondence from Schwartz & Earp Attorneys At Law to Sheriff Mike Sullivan; Reference Lizbeth A. Garrett – Estate of Maj. Chester Garrett; December 20, 1977
El Paso County Sheriff's Department Correspondence to Larry Schwartz; Reference Letter dated December 20, 1977; December 27, 1977

Chapter 18
Federal Bureau of Investigation Communique, Reference Donald Smith; May 15, 1977
Federal Bureau of Investigation Communique, Reference Donald Smith; May 18, 1977
El Paso County Sheriff's Department Investigative Report; May 17, 1977
El Paso County Sheriff's Department Investigative Report; May 19, 1977
El Paso County Sheriff's Department Investigative Report; May 20, 1977
El Paso County Sheriff's Department Investigative Report; May 27, 1977

Chapter 19
Documentation from the private collection of Reynaldo Cervantes Jr.

Chapter 20
Federal Law Enforcement Agency Investigative Report; June 29, 1977

Chapter 21
Documentation from the private collection of Reynaldo Cervantes Jr.

Chapter 22
Federal Law Enforcement Agency Investigative Report; May 28, 1977
Federal Law Enforcement Agency Investigative Report; June 25, 1977

Chapter 23
Federal Law Enforcement Agency Investigative Report; June 1977
Federal Law Enforcement Agency Investigative Report; June 25, 1977
Federal Law Enforcement Agency Investigative Report; June 27, 1977
Federal Law Enforcement Agency Investigative Report; June 29, 1977
Federal Law Enforcement Agency Investigative Report; July 5, 1977

Chapter 24
Department of the Army Headquarters; 4th Infantry Division; Distinguish Service Cross citation; General Orders # 4796; September 21, 1970
Chapter 25
Federal Law Enforcement Agency Investigative Report; July 3, 1977
Chapter 26
Federal Law Enforcement Agency Investigative Report; July 3, 1977
Federal Law Enforcement Agency Investigative Report; July 7, 1977
Chapter 27
U.S. Army Investigative Report; July 6, 1977
U.S. Army Investigative Report; July 9, 1977
Chapter 28
U.S. Army Investigative Report; July 11, 1977
Chapter 29
Department of the Army Headquarters; 101st Airborne Division (Airmobile); General Orders # 3484; April 26, 1971
Chapter 30
U.S. Army Investigative Report; July 13, 1977
U.S. Army Investigative Report; July 18, 1977
Federal Law Enforcement Agency Investigative Report; July 19, 1977
U.S. Army Investigative Report; July 20, 1977
Federal Law Enforcement Agency Investigative Report; July 22, 1977
U.S. Army Investigative Report; July 20, 1977
Letter from Dr. Vincent J.M. DiMaio; Southwestern Institute of Forensic Sciences; dated July 20, 1977
U.S. Army Investigative Report; July 25, 1977
Chapter 31
Federal Law Enforcement Agency Investigative Report; July 26, 1977
U.S. Army Investigative Report; November 1977
Federal Law Enforcement Agency Investigative Report; August 3, 1977
Federal Law Enforcement Agency Investigative Report; August 1, 1977
Federal Law Enforcement Agency Investigative Report; August 4, 1977
Federal Law Enforcement Agency Investigative Report; August 2, 1977
U.S. Army Investigative Report; August 3, 1977
U.S. Army Investigative Report; July 27, 1977
Chapter 32
Documentation from the private collection of Reynaldo Cervantes Jr.
Chapter 33
Federal Law Enforcement Agency Investigative Report; August 3, 1977
U.S. Army Investigative Report; August 3, 1977
U.S. Army Investigative Report; August 8, 1977
U.S. Army Investigative Report; January 19, 1978

Chapter 34
Documentation from the private collection of Reynaldo Cervantes Jr.
MIA Facts Site, Accounting for the Missing: Description of Activities to Account for the Missing in SE Asia; M. I. A.: Accounting for the Missing in Southeast Asia; by Paul D. Mather, LTC, USAF (Ret.); < http://www.miafacts.org/accntng.htm>
Chapter 35
U.S. Army Investigative Report; January 19, 1978
U.S. Army Investigative Report; January 19, 1978
Chapter 36
Headquarters Army Advisory Group; United States Military Assistance Command, Vietnam; General Orders # 17; January 3, 1973
Chapter 37
Federal Law Enforcement Agency Correspondence; October 20, 1977
Chapter 38
U.S. Army Correspondence, Subject: Murder of Chester Garrett; November 30, 1977
U.S. Army Investigative Report; November 17, 1977
U.S. Army Investigative Report; January 19, 1978
Chapter 39
Federal Law Enforcement Agency Investigative Report; December 16, 1977
Chapter 40
Correspondence from Headquarters Army Advisory Group; United States Military Assistance Command, Vietnam; February 12, 1973
Translation of Republic of Vietnam Citation for Vietnamese Gallantry Cross with Gold Star; January 24, 1973
Chapter 41
U.S. Army Investigative Report; January 19, 1978
U.S. Army Investigative Report; January 23, 1978
Chapter 42
U.S. Army Correspondence from USAADCENFB; Subject: Recommendation for Award – Major Chester Garrett; January 31, 1977
Department of the Army, Headquarters, U.S. Army Air Defense Center and Fort Bliss; Permanent Orders 99-1; July 11, 1977
Chapter 43
U.S. Army Investigative Report; January 13, 1977
Chapter 44
El Paso Sheriff's Office Investigative Report; May 1, 2006
Chapter 45
El Paso Sheriff's Office Investigative Report; May 1, 2006

Chapter 46
Supplemental Serology\DNA Report; Texas Department of Public Safety, Regional Crime Laboratory, El Paso; February 26, 2007
Supplemental Serology\DNA Report; Texas Department of Public Safety, Regional Crime Laboratory, El Paso; March 26, 2007
Chapter 47
El Paso Sheriff's Office Investigative Report; June 3, 2006
Fax from Yahoo; dated June 12, 2006; invoice for email records
El Paso Sheriff's Office Investigative Report; June 12, 2006
Chapter 48
El Paso Sheriff's Office Investigative Report; August 9, 2006
Chapter 49
El Paso Sheriff's Office Investigative Report; May 5, 2011
Chapter 50
El Paso Sheriff's Office Investigative Report; January 17, 2012
Chapter 51
El Paso Sheriff's Office Investigative Report; January 5, 2013
El Paso Sheriff's Office Correspondence; January 8, 2013
Chapter 52
El Paso Sheriff's Office Investigative Report; January 13, 2013
Chapter 53
El Paso Sheriff's Office Investigative Report; January 23, 2013
Chapter 54
El Paso Sheriff's Office Investigative Report; January 5, 2013
El Paso Sheriff's Office Investigative Report; January 28, 2013
Chapter 55
Knoxville Police Department Incident Report; February 7, 2018
Chapter 56
El Paso Sheriff's Office Investigative Report; February 7, 2013
Chapter 57
El Paso Sheriff's Office Investigative Report; June 27, 2013
Chapter 58
Supplemental Forensic Biology Laboratory Report; Texas Department of Public Safety, Crime Laboratory, El Paso; May 7, 2013
Chapter 59
Personal Recollection of Detective Antonio Arias
Chapter 60
El Paso Sheriff's Office Investigative Report; June 16, 2013
Chapter 61
El Paso Sheriff's Office Investigative Report; July 2, 2013
Chapter 62
El Paso Sheriff's Office Investigative Report; August 27, 2013

Chapter 63
Roger Garrett's trial transcripts provided by the El Paso County District Attorney's Office
Chapter 64
Personal Recollection of Detective Antonio Arias
Martinez, Arron; El Paso Times; Trial begins for '77 murder – Man's body was found out in desert; October 16, 2015, page 1B-2B
Martinez, Arron; El Paso Times; Testimony evaluates gain; October 17, 2015, pages 1B-2B
Martinez, Arron; El Paso Times; More details emerge on 1977 murder; October 20, 2015, page 1B-2B
Martinez, Arron; El Paso Times; 1977 murder trial coming to a close; October 21, 2015, page 1B-2B
Martinez, Arron; El Paso Times; GARRETT FOUND GUILTY; October 22, 2015, page 1B-2B
Martinez, Arron; El Paso Times; Garrett gets prison time; October 23, 2015, page 1B, 5B

Character Index

Altshul, Samuel, Army CID	pages 11, 25
Anchondo, Irene, EPSO	pages 145, 179
Anderson, Elaine, 1LT	pages 21, 24, 34
Andrade, Jorge, EPSO	pages 165, 169, 176, 186
Arias, Antonio "Tony", EPSO	pages 138-149, 150-154, 156-159, 164-166, 168-172, 176-179, 181-183, 185-188, 191, 193, 195, 198, 203, 205, 207
Austin, Curtis	pages 88, 102, 112
Banuelos, John	pages 1-2, 9, 172
Barber, James, SP4	page 87
Beasley, Tania	pages 102, 105
Belknap, James, EPSO	pages 139-140, 149, 156, 158, 164-166, 168, 172, 179, 181, 203
Bell, Annitta	pages 84-85
Bell, Christopher, KPD	page 176
Belvin, Paul, SP4	page 84
Berry, Elaine	pages 64-65, 103, 188-189
Berry, Phillip	page 64
Bland, Theodore "Jerry", SP4	pages 72-74, 77, 84-88, 90-92, 102
Boggs, Elmo, SGT	pages 77, 85-86, 88-89
Borenstein, Frederick, M.D.	pages 9, 18, 44
Boyette, L. EPSD	page 2
Brown, Wallace, EPSD	pages 18, 20, 24-25, 36, 39, 42-43, 45, 58, 64, 92, 134
Brewington, Jonathan, PFC	page 84
Butterworth, Denise, ADA	pages 172, 193-194, 199, 203, 205-206
Butts, Jim, ADA	page 48
Cartlidge, Marion, SP4	page 46
Ceniceros, Christine, Texas DPS	pages 144, 156, 197, 199
Cervantes, Reynaldo	page 207-208
Chapman, Wally	page 44, 98
Chavez, Rafael, EPSO	page 179

Chavira, Edward, EPSO	page 183
Claudia, FNU, DIS	page 19
Cohen, Michael, Attorney	pages 56, 59, 61, 134-136, 181-182
Comee, William, COL	pages 48, 60, 109
Conner, Jackie	pages 139-142, 178, 206
Contin, Juan, MD	pages 197, 205
Cooley, Lawrence, SSG	pages 72-73
Cooper, Herbert, Attorney	page 127
Cooper, Kenneth, FBI	pages 66, 112
Courtois, Edward, SSG	pages 44, 93-94, 98
Courtois, Kathleen	pages 44, 93-94, 98
Cowan, John, ADA	pages 48, 51-52, 55, 58, 61, 134-136
Crossmon, Wallace, FBI	pages 111-112
Darby, William, GEN	page 76
Davis, Rodney, FBI	page 90
Dekoatz, Matthew, Attorney	pages 193-194, 196-203
Devaney, Katherine	pages 170, 191
Diaz, Manuel, MD	page 9
Dickson, Sherine	page 102
Diggs, Isaac, CPT	pages 24-25, 115
DiMaio, Vincent, MD	page 107
Domeny, Gary, Army CID	pages 9, 12
Drake, Debbie	pages 170, 186-187, 193-194
Echols, Ann	page 97
Ellington nee Smith, Cheryl	pages 39, 42, 110, 141, 147-149
Esper, Richard, Attorney	page 205
Farr, David, CPT	pages 106-107
Fowkes, John, FBI	page 111
Franzoni, Steve, SFA	page 208
Gabbert, Gary, EPSO	pages 152-153, 164, 169, 187
Garress, Gayle, EPSD	page 34
Garrett, Dino	page 142
Garrett nee Francis, Adina	pages 7, 143

Garrett, Sabrina	pages 170, 191
Garrett, Sidney	page 7
Garrett, Susan	pages 176-177, 200, 202-203
Gathright, Roderick, PFC	pages 85-91, 102, 106, 121, 125, 129, 133
Gee, James "J.W.", Army CID	pages 77, 85-86, 90, 92-94, 96, 98, 100-103, 105-107, 110-112, 115, 117, 121, 125-126, 129, 131, 133, 181
Gersa, Me, CPT	pages 12, 23
Gilman, Roger, CPT	pages 43, 58
Gomez, H.Y. "Chickie", EPSD	pages 12, 18, 43, 58, 64, 77, 85-86, 88, 134
Gooch, FNU, CPT	page 39
Gurrola, Manuel, EPSD	pages 11, 58, 134
Guyer, Rusty, AUSA	page 127
Hall, Agnes	page 94
Hall, Garnett "Garrett"	pages 66, 94
Hall, Harrell, LTC	pages 9-11, 19-20, 25, 35-36, 59-60, 67, 96-98, 107, 154-155, 173, 197
Hall, Jack, Army CID	pages 10-11, 18, 25, 34, 44, 64
Hammond, Joseph, SP5	pages 20, 100
Hawkins, Joe, 1stSGT	pages 19-20
Heffelfinger, Theresa	pages 169-170, 174, 194-195
Heide, FNU, MP	pages 44-45
Herrera, Mike, Judge	page 183
Hicks, Charles, SP4	pages 24, 35, 77, 79
Hill, Roosevelt, PV1	pages 20, 24-25, 77, 87 89-90, 100, 105, 115
Hornisher, Joseph, LTC	pages 117, 125
Hudspeth, Harry, Judge	page 121
Irons, Harlan, SGT	page 125
Jackson, Howard, SP4	pages 11-13, 25, 70, 74,

	84-88, 131, 133
Johnson, Mary	page 42
Jones, Abby	page 93
Juarez, Erlinda	pages 24, 26, 40, 92-93
Kangus, Ray, CW4	page 92
Kelly, Francis, COL	page 27
Kingston, Robert, GEN	page 119
Kunst, John, FBI	pages 71-72, 90
Larson, Matthew "Buddy"	pages 151, 160, 165
Laskow, Gregory, CPT	pages 98-99
Leal, Irma	pages 86, 112, 115
Leniger, FNU, MP	page 44
Lennox, Alan, NYHA	pages 71-72
Lirette, Anthony, Army CID	page 19
Lizarraga, Marcos, Judge	pages 193, 205
LNU, Sylvia	page 16
Lott, Willie, CPT	page 10
Loveland, Patricia	pages 166, 168, 174
Lyons, Daniel, FBI	pages 71-72
Magruder, Richard, SP5	page 34, 171
Malone, Orba, Attorney	page 36
Martin, George, SFC	pages 19-20
Martin, James, SGT	page 24
McCarthy, Donna	pages 98, 106
McClellan, John, CPT	page 116
McClellan, Karen, 1LT	pages 96, 101, 115-117
McClellan, Stan, GEN	page 96
McCoy, Barbara	page 42
McCrea, R.J., EPSD	pages 2, 8, 11
McDonald, Raymond, SFC	page 93
McGraw, Russell, COL	pages 26, 67
McKinley, Dianne	page 72-73
McKinley, Gil	page 72-73
McNeill, David, MAJ	page 64
McWilliams, Woodrow, CPT	page 111
Miller, Tom, MAJ	page 10
Mitchell, Ralph, MAJ	page 125
Molina, Jennifer, PFC	pages 12, 20-24, 26, 34-35, 39-40, 49-55, 58-

	59, 77-79, 84, 88-89, 93, 96-97, 100, 106, 171
Montemayor, Pedro "Pete", Texas DPS	pages 2, 8, 11-12, 19-20, 58, 134
Montoya, Bettie	pages 110-111, 126
Montoya, James, ADA	page 205
Morales, Ruben, Attorney	pages 193, 195, 203
Moses, Franklin, CSM	page 106
Myers, Kyle, ADA	pages 172, 193-195, 202-203
Myerson, Christine	pages 199-201
Nelson, Elizabeth	page 44
Nelson, Joseph	page 44
Omohundro, John, EPSD	pages 2, 8-9, 18-20, 24, 34-35, 58-59, 61, 66, 134, 179, 181-182, 193
Orrison, Steven, CPT	pages 18, 24, 100-101
Patterson, Jeanne	pages 166-168, 174, 194, 196
Phillips, William, NYHA	page 71
Pletcher, Jeroline "Jerrie"	pages 42-43, 111-113
Pletcher, J.J.	page 43
Polanco, Jerry	page 111
Ramos, Robert, Attorney	page 205
Rensen, Wayne	page 112
Resen, FNU, CPT	page 21
Reuter, Jim, EPSO	pages 150, 153
Reyes, Aldo	page 207
Reyes, Jesus "Chuy", EPSD	pages 2, 8-9, 11-12, 18, 21, 24, 34, 36, 42-43, 58, 61, 67, 73, 134, 156, 180, 197
Reyes, Silvestre, USBP	page 8
Reynolds, Bennett, SSG	pages 105
Rios, Joe, EPPD	pages 36, 42
Rivera, Rene, SSG	page 34
Roberts, John, SP4	page 28
Rozman, Joseph, CPT	pages 23, 34, 39

Rutherford, Bill, EPSD	pages 2, 8
Saenz, Rafael, Army CID	page 10
Santibanez, Louis, EPSO	pages 179, 188
Schwartz, Larry, Attorney	page 69
Serwatka, Stanley, AUSA	page 125
Shannon, Clarence, NYHA	page 71
Sherwin, Robert, 1LT	pages 10-11, 13, 24-25, 43, 113, 191-192
Simmons, Steve, ADA	page 170
Smith, Gretchen	pages 141, 143
Smith, David, SP5	pages 25, 86-87, 115
Smith, Donald	pages 70-74, 77, 84-92, 102, 105, 112, 121, 125, 127, 133
Smith, Frank	page 152
Smith, Loretta	pages 70-73
Smith nee Hall, Ruth	page 98
Smith, Tammy	page 146
Snelson, Harry	pages 67, 112
Snelson, Robert	pages 60, 65-67, 112, 115, 162, 199-200
Sorel, Fresnel	pages 72-74, 77, 84-85, 87-89, 91, 93, 102, 105-106, 112, 127
Stout, Mac, EPSD	pages 2, 8-9, 11, 19, 67, 135
Sullivan, Mike, Sheriff EPSD	pages 2, 8, 67, 69, 135
Thomas, Eugene, PFC	pages 11-13, 20, 24-25, 70, 74, 77, 84-87, 98, 105, 112, 115, 125, 131, 133
Timmons, Fred, EPSD	pages 2-3, 8-9, 11-12, 19-20, 34-36, 39, 44, 48, 58, 61, 64, 66-67, 70-73, 77, 84-86, 88, 112, 134-136, 172, 179, 182
Torres, Bertha "Birdie"	pages 86, 112, 115
Turner, Benny	page 43

Turner, Connie	pages 43, 45
Turner, Cory	page 43
Turner, Sharon	pages 42-43, 45, 110-113, 147
Vidmar, Maureen	pages 142, 146, 149
Washington, Jerome, EPSO	pages 154, 159, 164-165, 173, 179, 183, 185-186
Webb, Gary, FBI	pages 70-73, 77, 85-86, 88-90, 92, 96, 98, 121, 125-127, 129, 133
Wentzel, John & Mrs	pages 35, 39, 162
Westfall, Thomas, FBI	pages 36, 44, 66
Westmoreland, William, GEN	pages 31, 62
Whitehouse, John, MAJ	page 101
Willis nee Graham, Ardular "Dia"	pages 74, 85, 91-92
Willis, Bernard	page 91
Wilson, Pam	page 88
Wilson, Jackie, Army CID	page 109
Wilson, Verline	page 98
Yearwood, Reginald, EPSD	pages 2, 8-9, 18, 21, 34, 58, 179
Zazenski, Edward, CPT	page 34

Author Bios:

Antonio Arias, Reynaldo Cervantes Jr., and Eric Norway

Antonio "Tony" Arias was born and raised in El Paso, Texas. He retired from the El Paso Sheriff's Office after 32 years of dedicated service. Tony now spends his time with family and plans to continue his venture into writing.

Reynaldo Cervantes Jr. hails from San Antonio, Texas. After a brief stint in the US Army as an Intelligence Officer, Rey had a long and successful career in federal law enforcement in Intelligence. Rey currently researches military history and enjoys spending time with family and friends in South Texas and El Paso.

Eric Norway is a former Border Patrol Agent, retired DEA Special Agent/Pilot, and lives in El Paso, Texas. Eric enjoys writing, dabbling in aviation, hiking with his dogs and being with family.

Made in the USA
Coppell, TX
17 April 2020